Ulrich von Liechtenstein's
Service of Ladies

Translated by
J. W. THOMAS

With an introduction by
KELLY DeVRIES

THE BOYDELL PRESS

Introduction © Kelly DeVries 2004

Ulrich von Liechtenstein's Service of Ladies
translated in condensed form by J. W. Thomas.
The University of North Carolina Studies in the
Germanic Languages and Literatures, No. 63.
Copyright © 1969 by the University of North Carolina Press
This edition has been published by arrangement with the
University of North Carolina Press, Chapel Hill, North Carolina 27514, USA
www.uncpress.unc.edu.

First published 1969
The University of North Carolina Press

New Edition 2004

First Person Singular

Transferred to digital printing

ISSN 1743-4769

ISBN 978-1-84383-095-5

The Boydell Press is an imprint of Boydell & Brewer Ltd
PO Box 9, Woodbridge, Suffolk IP12 3DF, UK
and of Boydell & Brewer Inc.
668 Mt Hope Avenue, Rochester, NY 14620, USA
website: www.boydellandbrewer.com

A CiP catalogue record for this book is available
from the British Library

This publication is printed on acid-free paper

ULRICH VON LIECHTENSTEIN'S
SERVICE OF LADIES

Contents

THE *REAL* ULRICH VON LIECHTENSTEIN[1]

In the recent popular movie *A Knight's Tale* (Columbia Tristar Pictures, 2001), when Geoffrey Chaucer (Paul Bettany) heralds the tournament appearance of poor-squire-turned-tournament-champion William Thatcher (Heath Ledger) as Ulrich von Liechtenstein, a new cinematic hero was born. In the movie, Ulrich's tournament victories pile up and pile up until he wins the world championship against the great and extremely malevolent French champion, Count Adhemar (Rufus Sewell) . . . and, of course, he wins the noble girl, Jocelyn (Shannyn Sossamon). However, this was not the first Ulrich von Liechtenstein in history, nor could it ever be said that *A Knight's Tale's* Ulrich von Liechtenstein was more cinematic than the medieval one!

The real, the medieval Ulrich von Liechtenstein was born around 1200 however in Styria, in what today is southern Austria. He was the son of noble parents, hence the *von* in his name, but there is no record of his being the eldest son or heir to his father's nobility. Still, Ulrich's nobility meant that he would be well educated. This education consisted of all the arts and letters popular during his time, perhaps even the seven liberal arts. He certainly learned to read and write, in his own vernacular dialect if not also in Latin, and perhaps also in Medieval French and Italian. His own later writings were written in what is now called Middle High German, but show signs of a knowledge of these other Romance languages. Yet Ulrich von Liechtenstein would be schooled in other arts befitting his class and status. He would have learned martial arts: how to fight with different arms and armor, on horseback and on foot. Unlike many of his noble counterparts, Ulrich would combine all of this education together, providing the twenty-first century medieval enthusiast with an example of one of the most celebrated jousting poets or, perhaps, poetic jousters the world has ever known.

The early thirteenth century of Ulrich von Liechtenstein's youth was one of relative peace. The Crusades were still being fought, but after the fall of Constantinople to the Latin soldiers of the Fourth Crusade, later crusading endeavors became less European-wide and more individual. Crusades would still be waged, but by separate kings and princes, such as Emperor Frederick II and King Louis IX, and sometimes even without the permission of the papacy. This meant that the general call for western European Christian warriors to fight in the Holy Land which had always been sent previously from Rome was quieted. Noble soldiers were still required; no one who wished to participate on Crusade would be turned away. But there was certainly less pressure for men like Ulrich von Liechtenstein to travel to the Holy Land for much of their youth. Like other young warriors of his time and region, Ulrich appears to have promised to go on Crusade, but, also like these other young warriors, he never went.

There was also no warfare in Austria, Italy, Switzerland, or any of the southern German principalities during the early thirteenth century. This was a good thing, of course, and quite rare for the Middle Ages. But it also meant that young would-be warriors had difficulty in practicing their martial arts. It also meant that many of them had few ways of acquiring knighthood, their most sought after goal. Most, it is true, would have served their fathers, uncles, cousins, or, perhaps, non-relatives as pages and squires. But they would usually have needed to show some type of valor during combat to earn their knightly spurs. At times a special occasion might suffice to allow young men unable to prove themselves in warfare to become a knight. So it was for Ulrich von Liechtenstein. As a young boy he served as a page, and as a young man as a squire, the latter between 1215 and 1219 to the Markgraf (or Marquis) Heinrich von Istria. And in 1222, at the occasion of his daughter's marriage, Duke Leopold of Austria, granted Ulrich von Liechtenstein's greatest wish when he made him, and 199 other young warriors, a knight.

Where young thirteenth-century knights and squires practiced their skills during times of peace, and sometimes also during times of war, was the tournament. A tournament might be held for any reason, sometimes to celebrate a special event and sometimes only to hold a sporting event. Actually, there was not a single "tournament" at this time, but a number of different types of tournament. One of these types was the mélée. This really was the tournament proper, where two "armies" vied against each other in a mock battle fought on a tournament plain. These armies would consist of both cavalry and infantry soldiers; even archers might take part. All weapons could be permitted in this mock battle, although of course they would be blunted. A cavalry charge would initiate the mélée, with further warfare between all of the forces continuing until one "army" was declared the victor.

A second type of tournament was the joust or tilt. This was a one-on-one combat fought on horseback. It also generally took part on a tournament field, although this field would of necessity be narrowed until there was but a double lane divided by a barrier. The jousters would approach each other on opposite sides of this barrier, dropping their lances at the last moment in an effort to break them against their opponent's armor. Points would be given for whether and where these lances struck, and special effects — lances breaking in a "cinematic" way — might bring extra points. Unfortunately, no thirteenth-century lance has survived, but it is known that they were blunted. Some historians also wonder if sometimes these weapons were not cut or trimmed by their users in order to increase the effect.

Although single jousts were known, in a tournament situation several jousts would be held during which the participants might be decreased as they lost. Ultimately, only the final two jousters would face off against each other in one final match to decide the tournament championship. Every rider would therefore need to fight several jousts before he could win the top prize, which was generally given by the tournament sponsors, although often awards were given by the participants to their victors in the form of ransom for their "lost" horses and armor. In some tournaments the more professional jousters might be "seeded", meaning that they would be able to skip some of the preliminary rounds of the meet.

Of course, each tournament participant would wear their finest armor, in this case a full coat of chain armor covering all extremities, with chain-mail mittens and boots to cover the hands and feet, and a mail coif to cover the neck and head. Atop this would sit the warrior's helmet, likely a Great Helm. He would also carry a shield; on this and on his horse's barding would be his heraldic decoration, identifying the rider's nobility and lineage. This can be seen in Ulrich von Liechtenstein's portrait painted as a manuscript illumination during the early fourteenth century by an anonymous illustrator (Heidelberg, Universitätsbibliothek, MS Cod. pal. Germ 848, f.237; see cover illustration) which, although painted later, fairly correctly portrays the arms, armor, and even possibly the heraldry of the previous century.

Ulrich von Liechtenstein was a champion jouster. How do we know? Because he told us. This should not be seen as egotistical, however. Chroniclers might be interested enough to record the holding of a tournament and the event which prompted it, but they rarely report the participants or even the winners. Instead, most of the great jousters of the day are mentioned in chivalric tales, poems and prose romances, which almost as a matter of course included at least one tournament. Ulrich von Liechtenstein not only appears in one of these, but in fact he wrote it. And it was quite good, and seemingly quite popular. Its title is *Frauendienst*, or in English translation, *The Service of Women*.

Ulrich von Liechtenstein is the hero of *Frauendienst*. In it he tells his story, as a knight and a jouster. As a boy of twelve Ulrich fell in love, or at least he realized that the greatest happiness and honor for a knight came in the service of a woman, so Ulrich chose one. She was a beautiful noble woman, older and more noble than he was, and she was married, but in the tales of love and chivalry that hardly mattered. What did matter was that she initially spurned his advances. Of course, Ulrich von Liechtenstein was still a child at the time so this did not come as a surprise to him, but he also used this rejection, in the way so may other authors had done and would continue to do, to recognize that his goal, the winning of his lady's heart, would come only after a life full of obstacles, frustrations, and adventures. He would have to earn her love.

From age twelve to age seventeen, as he grew into manhood, Ulrich von Liechtenstein adored this lady from afar. He managed to stay close by her, however, by becoming a page in her court. As such, he was able to touch what she touched and cherish the things that were hers. He writes that sometimes he stole into her chamber after she had bathed so that he could wash his hands in her water; on some of these occasions he would even drink from her bath.

Once he learned to joust he found that he had a new means of expressing his love for his lady. He would enter tournaments wearing her colors. It is hard to know at this stage if his unnamed love interest was aware of Ulrich's advances. Certainly she must have seen Ulrich von Liechtenstein, once her page, wearing her colors and participating in tournaments. She may even have seen him stealing out of her chamber after her baths. If so, she did nothing to encourage his continuing interests, but little also to stop them. That was until, after he had gained a few tournament victories, Ulrich asked his niece to approach the lady as a mouthpiece for his affection. His lady would not listen to Ulrich's love appeals. She told his niece that she was repulsed by her uncle's appearance, that he had a harelip, and that he was lower-born than she.

Such a rejection still did not stop Ulrich von Liechtenstein's pursuit of the lady. He had his harelip removed by surgery, recuperated — for six weeks — and wrote a love song for her. This softened her a little, and she allowed Ulrich to attend a riding party in which she was present, indicating to him that should he ride close to her they might have a chance to talk. He joined the party but when he rode close to his beloved he became so nervous that he could not say a word to her. Again she spurned him, this time tearing a lock from his hair to emphasize her rejection of him.

Ulrich von Liechtenstein returned to the tournament circuit, all the time fighting not only for victories in the mélée and joust but also fighting for the love of this beautiful woman. But for three years she would not even allow him to fight in her name nor to carry her colors. He constantly sent her letters and poems, but these were ridiculed and rejected by her. In one letter he claimed that he had wounded a finger in a joust fought that day; she derided him, saying that he exaggerated the severity of his wound. In response, Ulrich cut off one of fingers and sent it to her. With this gesture, his lady finally gave in, writing back that she would look at his severed digit every day and remember the sacrifice he had made for her.

Having won some affection from her, Ulrich von Liechtenstein determined that an even larger display would win her over entirely. He decided that he would fight a series of jousts from Venice to the borders of Bohemia. This he called the *Venusfahrt* (Venus Journey), in honor of that goddess of love and of all women. To further spotlight this trek, Ulrich would dress as "Lady Venus" both in the joust and when not fighting. He does not record how he pulled off such a stunt, although he does insist that no one saw through his feminine disguise. However unlikely this was, and Ulrich does write that his appearance as Venus at times aroused quite a bit of laughter, the chance to fight a joust interested many nobles along his path. During the five week period of the *Venusfahrt* Ulrich claims to have broken 307 lances with opponents, fighting sometimes eight jousts in a day. Should an opponent be successful in breaking his lance on Ulrich, in other words actually hitting Ulrich's armor, he would be presented with a ring. 271 of these rings were awarded during his journey.

At the end of his *Venusfahrt* Ulrich von Liechtenstein returned to his lady, hoping that his spectacle would have appealed to her. She knew that he had undertaken the *Venusfahrt*, and she had sent word to Ulrich that she wished to speak with him. However, she instructed the love-smitten knight to come to her dressed as a leper and to sit with the other lepers begging outside her door. When he was so attired she passed by Ulrich but did not greet him, instead making him sleep outside in the rain. The next morning she sent a message to this "beggar" that he could climb the rope to her bedroom window, but, after he had further fulfilled her instructions by wading across a lake, as he ascended the rope his lady unhooked it and Ulrich fell into the foul moat below. Ultimately, it was only after Ulrich von Liechtenstein promised his lady that he would go on Crusade in her name and began to prepare for such a venture that she called it off and offered him her love.

What symbols, tokens, or acts these were is not indicated by Ulrich in *Frauendienst*. One hopes that it was worth it in the end, for the poor knight, it seems, had been made to perform the most difficult of tasks to earn this woman's favors. However, it was not as if he was without female companionship. It appears that Ulrich von Liechtenstein was married throughout most of these chivalric displays. On one occasion during the *Venusfahrt* he stopped off for three days to be with his wife. He also reports that she was quite good at managing his estate and raising his children. So there must have been something more. His lady had become a symbol for the great jouster. She was a symbol of the honor and love for women that he held as such a principle for his and seemingly every other young nobleman's life.

Then there was the tournament. His lady became a means for Ulrich von Liechtenstein to participate in tournaments. This was a sporting pastime that not only displayed chivalric valor and fighting skill, but it was fun, too! It appears that young knights of Ulrich's ilk wanted to fight mélées and jousts whenever and wherever they could. So enthusiastic were they, Ulrich writes, that when, gathered together for negotiations between the lords of Istria and Neustria, the opportunity arose to joust at Freisach in May 1224, at Ulrich's urging, the peace conference was held up until a full-scale tournament could be organized.

By the *Venusfahrt*, Ulrich von Liechtenstein had given up the mélée. He was too good and too well known to participate in that form of tournament any longer. Although well armored, tournament injuries could still happen, and it is clear that as a well-known jouster Ulrich may have been singled out for particular attention by any number of younger men willing to gain their own renown at the expense of his own. This may also have been the reason why he fought the *Venusfahrt* in disguise. Still, it is difficult to know how anyone could miss the great jousting knight's style of fighting on the tiltyard. Nor does it seem that they could miss the participation of his entourage in the processions leading up to the jousts which he was to fight in. In these processions large heraldic banners would be flown, musicians would play, squires would bear lances, and knights would parade through town to the tournament field. At Neunkirchen during the *Venusfahrt*, Ulrich reports, more than one hundred knights, their squires and banners, marched and rode to the tournament. At times the procession was not large, such as at Korneuburg, also during his *Venusfahrt*, only a single bugler and one banner paraded before him onto the field, although then, perhaps in order to make this procession longer, Ulrich had his pieces of armor also carried in piece by piece.

In later life Ulrich von Liechtenstein continued to joust. In 1240 he organized another large series of jousts which he called the *Artusfahrt* (Journey for Arthur) in which he would again joust against all comers. The jousters would naturally not fight under their own names but instead would carry the names of Arthur's greatest knights, Gawain, Lancelot, etc. Should an opponent break three lances against him, he would have a right to join Ulrich's "Round Table," a special chivalric circle the joining of which would bring the honor that later in the Middle Ages would be reserved for members of Chivalric Orders such as the Golden Fleece or the Garter. Again Ulrich von Liechtenstein traveled throughout the lands near to his home, jousting to his and his opponents' hearts' content; on one occasion, at Neustadt, after the *Artusfahrt* joust was set up for a fortnight's time, the intervening time was spent by Ulrich and his fellow knights, of course, in jousting. Unfortunately, the final joust of the Artusfahrt was delayed and then banned altogether by Duke Frederick of Austria. His reasoning: political events meant a need for cautious sobriety rather than celebratory sport.

In later life, when he had retired from jousting, Ulrich von Liechtenstein played several minor political roles in Styria and Austria. As an administrative official, a *ministerialis*, Ulrich had some power to wield, although not enough to strike out on his own. Instead, he submitted to those whom he wisely thought could benefit and protect him. In 1250 this was the archbishop of Salzburg, with whom Ulrich made a military treaty to provide soldiers and castles for the archbishop; in return, Ulrich gained the archbishop's blessing of the marriage between two of Ulrich's children and two of the archbishop's richest ministeriales' children. In one of these marriages, Ulrich von Liechtenstein's son and heir, Ulrich, married Cunegunde of Goldegg, the daughter of the rich and powerful Conrad of Goldegg, thereby ensuring his father's name and legacy. Liechtenstein today remains as free and independent as its jousting namesake so many years before.

Was this all true? Did Ulrich von Liechtenstein really take part in all of the tournaments he said he did, sometimes dressed as Venus and sometime calling himself Arthur? Do we really care? After all, half the fun of having a cinematic hero, in this case the real Ulrich von Liechtenstein, is not knowing if all his adventures are real or fiction.

---

[1]This article originally appeared in *Medieval History Magazine*, 1 (Sept 2003), 34–39. Because of the medium, no footnotes appeared with the article originally; nor was there a bibliography with the article, except in the Middle High German edition of *Frauendienst* (ed. Franz Viktor Spechtler [Göppingen: Kümmerle, 1987]), and a modern German translation of it by same Middle High German editor (Klagenfurt: Wieser Verlag, 2000). This is because, despite the interesting character that Ulrich von Liechtenstein was historically and literally, despite the existence of the famous manuscript illumination depiction of him, portrayed with his rather exaggerated female headpiece (Heidelberg, Universitätsbibliothek, Ms. Cod. pal. Germ. 848, f.327), and despite the fact that nearly every historian of chivalry refers to Ulrich and his role in the history of tournaments and jousting, not much more is known about him than he writes about himself. Of course, this, as every historian knows, means that the credibility of the source is somewhat suspect. Or does it just add to the playfulness of a medieval tale understood in the atmosphere of merriment and celebration, as all historical, literary, and artistic sources suggest the tournaments were supposed to be?

For a recent collection of studies on Ulrich von Liechtenstein's literary corpus see *Ich, Ulrich von Liechtenstein: Literatur und Politik im Mittelalter: Akten der Akademie Friesach "Stadt und Kultur im Mittelalter," Friesach (Kärnten), 2–6, September 1996*, ed. Franz Viktor Spechtler and barbara Maier (Klagenfurt: Wieser, 1999). On the history of chivalry and tournaments see Maurice Keen, *Chivalry* (New Haven: Yale University Press, 1984); Richard Barber, *The Knight and Chivalry*, 2nd ed. (Woodbridge: The Boydell Press, 1975); Richard Barber, *The Reign of Chivalry* (New York: St. Martin's Press, 1980); Richard Barber and Juliet Barker, *Tournaments: Jousts, Chivalry and Pageants in the Middle Ages* (New York: Weidenfeld and Nicolson, 1989); and *Das ritterliche Turnier im Mittelalter: Beiträge zu einer vergleichenden Formen- und Verhaltensgeschichte des Ritertums*, ed. Josef Fleckenstein (Göttingen, Vandenhoeck & Ruprecht, 1985).

SERVICE OF LADIES

1   I greet the ladies, one and all,
    though my reward was ever small
    for serving them, I must confess.
    What wealth of virtue they possess!
    They're all the world can have of bliss,
    for God made nothing else like this:
    a noble woman. That is why
    my praise of them must be so high.

2   You must admit it, for it's true,
    none give the honor that is due
    to woman's goodness, though their praise
    outstrips the light of summer days.
    Where does the sunlight start and end?
    If one on whom I can depend
    can tell me that, then I'll declare
    that he has travelled everywhere.

3   Their splendor lights up every land;
    I do not know what distant strand
    may mark the limit of their splendor!
    Each word must change and be more tender,
    each passing year must leave the earth
    more fair before a woman's worth
    and goodness can be rightly heard,
    completely told in song and word.

4   How can the story be completed
    and all their virtues fully treated?
    There is no end of what to say.
    And when the world shall pass away
    the praise of women shall suffice
    for poets up in paradise.
    I fear, although I wish to speak
    their praise, my thoughts are all too weak.

5   Women are pure, refined are they,
    women are beautiful and gay,
    women can still love's deepest pain,
    women are never cruel and vain,
    women make kind and noble men.
    Well for him who deserves it when
    the women greet him as a friend!
    His sorrow and distress will end.

1

6   Women are rich in charm and grace.
To match their lovely form and face
is more than angels hope to do.
A woman, virtuous and true,
who has no faults of any kind,
must have an angel's heart and mind
and like an angel seems to glow.
You have my word that this is so.

7   My praise is finished. Now I plan
to tell a tale as best I can
and pray to God as I begin
that I may interest you therein,
that all will listen as one should,
and all of you will think it good.
My labors then will satisfy.
I swear the story is no lie.

8   When I was still a little child
my fancy often was beguiled
by what the poets sang and read
and what the wise men always said:
that none win fame who do not serve
good women as they all deserve,
but he who serves them with his sword
and heart receives a rich reward.

9   This I heard the wise men say:
none can be happy, none can stay
contented in this world but he
who loves and with such loyalty
a noble woman that he'd die
if it would save her from a sigh.
For thus all men have loved who gain
the honor others can't obtain.

10   I was a child when they spoke so
and knew no more than children know,
a hobbyhorse was still my steed;
I was so simple then indeed,
I thought, "Since lovely women raise
a man to such esteem and praise,
I'll serve the ladies faithfully
however it may go with me.

11   "I'll give my body, all my mind,
and life itself to womankind
and serve them all the best I can.
And when I grow to be a man
I'll always be their loyal thane;
though I succeed or serve in vain
I'll not despair and never part
from them," thus spoke my childish heart.

12   While lost in thoughts like these I grew
to twelve—I swear it all is true.
I pondered everywhere I went
just as my youthful fancy bent,
and, asking questions, rode around
wherever ladies could be found.
Their ways, the customs they enjoy
I learned while I was still a boy.

13   Whoever spoke of women's praise
I followed, just to hear each phrase,
for it would make my heart so light
and fill me with a true delight.
I heard from many a learned tongue
their excellence and honor sung;
they praised one here and praised one there,
they praised the ladies everywhere.

14   I heard the virtues of them all
but there is one whom I recall
whose fame was spread on every hand.
The best of singers in the land
commended her and her alone.
To whom her excellence was known,
who knew her virtue and good name,
would have to join in her acclaim.

16   She was extolled by knight and sage.
I later was the lady's page
and served her gladly four years through—
what I am telling you is true.
My youthful eyes could never see
a thing in her which should not be,
for she was always kind and good,
the very flower of womanhood.

3

17   My heart then spoke to me and said,
"Dearest friend, if you are led
to yield yourself to woman's spell
and only live to serve her well,
then she alone will ever do.
This counsel I must give to you:
since she's the one whom all prefer
we ought to go and live with her."

18   "I'll do, my heart, as you advise,
but do you think it would be wise
for us to labor for the pay
that lovely women give away?
This woman whom I am to serve
is far beyond what we deserve.
She is too high for us, we'll gain
but little for our work and pain.

20   "Heart, I'll swear an oath to this:
as I may gain eternal bliss,
I love her more than all the rest
and more than self. At your request
and in the hope that I may win
her affection, I'll begin
to serve my love this very day
and ever after, come what may."

21   My heart and body then conspired
to win the prize which both desired.
I went to her with longing sighs
and looked at her with loving eyes.
I thought with joy, "Can this be she
to whom I give my loyalty,
with whom I'll stay while I have breath,
who'll bring me happiness or death!"

22   I thought, "What can I do for her
that will induce her to prefer
me to the other noble boys
whom she presently employs?
If one should serve her better here
then I would be despised, I fear.
I just don't know what else to do
but serve her late, and early too."

24   Many times in summer hours
I would gather pretty flowers
in fields and meadows, everywhere,
and bring them to my lady fair.
If she should take them in her hand
my joy was all that I could stand.
I thought, "Your fingers hold each stem
just where I was holding them."

25   Great was my happiness when I
could be with others standing by
at meals and see the water poured
on those white hands which I adored.
I took the water secretly
with which she washed away with me
and, filled with love, I drank it all;
because of this my grief was small.

26   I served her as a child, but well
and more than I can ever tell.
Whate'er a child can do or may
I did for her until the day
my father took me home again.
I learned of longing sadness then
and knew the pain within my heart
that lovers feel when they must part.

27   I had to leave but, unresigned,
my stubborn heart remained behind
and would not go with me from there.
That surely was a strange affair,
that I should rule my body so
but could not force my heart to go.
It stayed with her both night and day
and had no rest from sad dismay.

28   Wherever I might walk or ride
my heart was always by her side,
and through the day and all night long
my love for her remained so strong
that I beheld her constantly.
Such was the love she won from me.
No matter what the time or place,
within my heart I saw her face.

29   I'll speak no more of this. It brought
me misery with every thought.
While thus my heart and body warred
I went to serve the noble lord
of Istria, a knight whose worth
was not surpassed in all the earth.
Margrave Henry was his name;
his virtue well deserved its fame.

31   He lived for honor; none has heard
him ever speak an evil word.
He was merry, he was bold,
his knightly traits were manifold.
He was loyal, he was true,
and he was honest, through and through.
He worshipped God and helped his friend;
so lived the prince until the end.

33   He helped me, still a simple lad,
to gain the knowledge which he had:
to talk with ladies and, of course,
to ride with skill on any horse,
to write sweet phrases in a letter —
he said, "I know of nothing better;
it shows a young man is refined
when he speaks well of womankind.

34   "Sweet words when joined to noble deeds
are what a noble lady needs.
I speak the truth and nothing less,
that you can never have success
with high-born ladies if you try
to flatter with an empty lie.
You'll gain no more than disbelief
and all your hopes will come to grief."

35   Had I been able to fulfil
such noble deeds as was his will,
I'd surely be a better man.
The years passed by as they began —
four years I longed for her and sighed.
While I was there my father died
and I went home, as those must do
whom parents leave possessions to.

36   My lord then gave me leave, and sent
me forth so well equipped I went
as proud as he, and looked as fine.
I travelled then to Liechtenstein,
my childhood home in Steierland.
I found there many a youthful band
which jousted. This was custom still;
so young men learned this knightly skill.

37   When I found them jousting there
I knew how I might win the fair
and charming one whose love I sought.
"If I'm to serve her," so I thought,
"I'll do it as an errant knight.
With sword and lance I'll boldly fight
for her each day and never waver.
God grant that I may win her favor."

39   I rode to many a tournament
and tilted everywhere I went.
Three years I wandered with my steed
and then became a knight indeed.
It happened in Vienna where
a feast was held beyond compare,
a wedding festival so grand
that thousands came from every land.

40   Prince Leopold of Austria gave
his lovely daughter to a brave
and noble Saxon who desired
her for his wife whom all admired.
The festival would suit a queen;
the like of it I've never seen
at any wedding anywhere.
It's nothing but the truth, I swear.

41   Those whom the worthy prince invited—
two hundred fifty squires—were knighted
with all due honor at the feast.
He gave a thousand knights, at least:
vassals, barons, even counts,
gold and silver, clothes and mounts.
The prince did this, and all could see
therein his noble majesty.

42   Five thousand knights and maybe more
ate from the goodly prince's store.
After melees dances came
and many another knightly game.
The duchess and her retinue
were there, her charming daughter, too.
The host of lovely ladies' eyes
upon us made our spirits rise.

43   The light of all my joy was there,
my sweet and faultless lady fair.
I saw her whom my heart preferred
but still I could not say a word
to her throughout the feast we had;
because of this I long was sad.
The watchers would not let it be;
their spying quite discouraged me.

44   But when the sweet and lovely charmer
saw me mounted, clad in armor,
she addressed a friend of mine,
"I think that it is really fine
that yon Sir Ulrich was among
those knighted. While still very young
he was my page, some years ago —
the Knight of Liechtenstein, you know."

45   Later, when my friend told me
and I found out how greatly she
was pleased, then I was happy, too,
and wondered thus, "Would she have you
to serve her as a faithful knight?"
The thought itself was true delight;
it was sweet and it was good —
I felt as proud as a young knight could.

46   Then came the festival's last day
and each one went his separate way
merrily from land to land.
Tournaments on every hand
to honor ladies were begun.
I could not miss a single one
but splintered lances everywhere
because I loved my lady fair.

47 I rode about and could attend
    twelve tourneys ere the summer's end,
    and there was many a cavalier
    of note with whom I broke a spear.
    'T was then I grew to man's full strength
    and learned the nightly skills at length
    so I was never overthrown.
    For this I thank my love alone.

48 The joys of summer disappeared
    as soon as icy winter neared.
    Then I was forced, although so ill
    with love, to cease my warlike drill—
    I'd suffered little pain thereby.
    I now was sad and knew not why.
    A longing sorrow came to me
    and seldom let my heart be free.

49 I felt the pangs of love in vain
    and could not tell her of my pain,
    which often filled my heart with woe.
    My ladylove was guarded so
    that never did I have a chance
    to tell her with a word or glance
    that I had always loved her best,
    more than myself and all the rest.

50 They would not let me see her ever,
    and so it was that I could never
    disclose to her what I would say.
    This made me sadder, day by day,
    like any other lovesick man.
    I had no messenger or plan
    to tell her what my wishes were
    and of the love I had for her.

51 Shall I reveal my suffering
    and not conceal a single thing:
    she didn't even know that I
    was serving her with deed and sigh.
    I often went to bed in sorrow
    and nursed my pain until the morrow,
    arose still burdened down with care
    and took it with me everywhere.

52   I was the gloomiest of men,
but only hear what happened when
I stopped once at a citadel.
The master there received me well
with all the honor that was due.
His wife, my aunt, was friendly, too.
"My dearest nephew," she spoke thus,
"you are most welcome here with us."

53   My aunt soon took me by the hand.
I followed at her soft command
to where no one could hear a word.
Now listen, this is what I heard:
"I'm pleased to see you once again;
now won't you tell me how you've been?
Have you been feeling good, or bad?
If you've been happy, I am glad."

54   She smiled and said, "You make me laugh;
what women say on your behalf
I'll tell you, though you shouldn't know.
I travelled several days ago
to see a friend, a lady who,
while we were talking, mentioned you.
She asked how you and I were kin
and I explained the truth therein.

55   "She then continued, 'It's been said,
. . . . . [*line missing*] . . . . .
that this young knight speaks always good
of women, as a noble should.
He'd like to serve, the rumor goes,
a certain lady whom he knows.
His service, should it prove a fact,
will surely be a knightly act.'

56   " I spoke, ' 'T was also said to me
that he admires a lady. She
is more to him than all the rest,
more than the life within his breast.
But who she is, I cannot say,
although he praises her each day
and tells that she is good and kind
and has a pure and noble mind.'

57
"Suddenly she begged that I
should speak at once with you and try
to learn her name whom you prefer.
I ask because I promised her
and said, I'd quickly let her know
and would not wait or let it go.
Now save me, nephew, from her blame
and tell me, what's the lady's name?"

58
"But, auntie, you should know full well,
the lady's name I'll never tell—
at least I won't till I have heard
you promise not to breathe a word
to anyone of this affair.
And also I must hear you swear
that you will be my messenger
and make my service known to her."

59
"I'll bear no messages for you
but I will swear, whate'er I do,
by God and all my hopes of bliss,
I'll never say a word amiss;
for you deserve as much, I'm sure.
With me her name will be secure.
If I can help in any way
all you need to do is say."

60
"I must tell you, I'm afraid,
for I can really use your aid.
It's this lady friend of yours
whom indeed my heart adores,
who's my delight and my desire,
she who asked you to inquire
what my lady's name might be;
that best of women, it is she."

61
"I can't believe what you have said—
dear friend, you've truly been misled.
For you she's much too highly born;
you'll only gain her wrath and scorn.
You cannot be successful there,
so hear my counsel and forbear.
It's best that you give up this thought
of serving her. 'T will come to naught."

62   "Whether joys or cares come thronging,
      I'm so overcome with longing
      and love that I shall have to try
      to serve her, even though I die
      while in her service. You will find
      that you can never change my mind.
      I'll serve my lady with each breath
      and faithfully until my death.

63   "If you won't come to my support
      or render aid of any sort
      then all my joy will turn to pain
      and life itself will be in vain.
      Would you prevent such misery,
      then you must tell her this from me:
      It's she I love. Without design
      I offer her this heart of mine."

64   "Nephew, what more is there to say?
      God grant that you will get your way
      and that the lady will be kind.
      I'll tell her what is on your mind
      and not withhold a single thing.
      In several hours I can bring
      your message and can tell her of
      your wish to serve her and your love."

65   "In reverence at your feet I kneel.
      Lady, I shall always feel
      thankful if your lips will tell
      my lady I shall serve her well,
      that I shall be her own true knight,
      and that my heart and soul and might
      belong to her. I'll freely give
      them all as long as I shall live.

66   "I've sung a new and pretty song
      of her, which you must take along
      with you and bring it to her ear
      and, on returning, let me hear
      if she believes the song is good.
      I praise her always, as I should
      and as I've done since I was young.
      Her virtues can't be fully sung.

"God bless you, aunt, for what you do."
"I hope He does the same for you."
"Now you must do your best for me."
"Trust only in my loyalty."
"By your leave, I now must go."
"May God protect you, friend." And so
I parted from my aunt, but sent
this song with her before I went.

THIS IS THE FIRST DANCE TUNE

No one can tell all about
a woman's goodness. Days ago
my heart began to blossom out.
She frees me from the cares I know
when, dressed in all her finery,
she walks along in front of me.
No angel is more fair than she.

By storm a woman seized my heart
and I must always be her knight.
Her form is lovely, every part;
her greeting fills me with delight.
All one could wish in her I find;
she leaves the others far behind
or I'm no judge of womankind.

You have shown more friendliness
to me than ever I deserve
You alone, I now confess,
are she whom I shall ever serve.
I'm always happy on the day
I see you, more than I can say.
My heart is joyful then and gay.

All the cheer that now is mine
I owe to no one else but you.
You are dear, without design,
and I would serve you and be true.
If you'll permit I'll show you how
I'll give away my freedom now.
I'll serve you faithfully. I vow.

68   I journeyed on with spirits high
and reasoned thus, "As long as I
have found a messenger to go
for me and let my lady know
about my wishes and my vow,
why, I can be lighthearted now
and need not sorrow anymore
and be much gayer than before.

69   And so I travelled unconcerned—
it wasn't long till I returned.
Five weeks I visited about
and in this time, as I found out,
my aunt had kept her word to me,
had made the trip and gone to see
my lady and was back again.
I soon received a message then.

70   It pleased me much, without delay
I rode to learn what she would say.
My aunt was kind to me and good,
receiving me as all friends should.
"I did what you insisted on,"
she said, "but wish I hadn't gone.
For, though I did what I could do,
I've been no help at all to you.

71   "Now just sit down beside me here;
I'll tell you very soon, my dear,
every single thing we said
so you can never be misled,
what she to me and I to her.
I was a faithful messenger
and told her that you loved her best,
more than yourself and all the rest.

74   "I said much more; before I closed
I read the song which you composed.
Then spoke your charming lady fair,
'It really is a pretty air,
but one he might as well have kept;
his service I cannot accept
and want to hear no more of this.
The topic we shall now dismiss.

75   " 'Your nephew may be a worthy man;
I'll grant him this and all I can.
I know him; at an early age
he came and lived here as a page,
and to his credit I can tell
he served me loyally and well.
But I insist he keep his peace.
Requests like that will have to cease.'

77   " 'But, lady, they should not provoke
your anger,' thus I quickly spoke,
'for young men often want and love
an object they're not worthy of.
They show their honor by their goal:
the high desire, the lofty soul,
and say a knight should prove his worth
by wooing one of noble birth.'

80   " 'That he excels I'll take your word
(although it's more than I have heard)
in every virtue, every skill,
yet for a woman it must still
prevent a close relationship
to see his most unsightly lip.
You must forgive my saying so:
it isn't pretty, as you know.'

81   "She wouldn't listen anymore.
I counsel you as once before,
let her wishes be your guide;
since she has such exalted pride
let her remain of service free
however dear your honor be.
Forget about her and display
a lofty soul another way."

82   "I cannot follow your advice,
dear aunt, for I would sacrifice
such fervent hopes that she'll be kind;
no words will ever change my mind.
This counsel you should never give
to me; I'll serve her while I live
and only bitter death shall part
me from the one who holds my heart."

83 "Well I'll not help, make no mistake."
"No, auntie dear, for Heaven's sake
you mustn't give me up this way.
Now listen to what I've got to say:
I'll have a doctor operate
upon my mouth. I shall not wait
and do not fear the consequence
since it's the cause of such offense."

85 "This I beg you not to do;
why it could be the death of you!
Live as God wanted you to live
and take whatever He may give
as being best for you and right;
this is the spirit of a knight.
To want what God does not ordain
reveals a spirit much too vain."

86 "God bless you, aunt, but I'm afraid
that my decision has been made.
Be sure, no matter how things go,
I'll not neglect to let you know.
I'll send you quickly any news
and only ask that you will lose
no time in giving it to her,
yourself, or by a messenger."

87 "I'll do it, nephew, this I swear,
but how I wish that you'd forbear
and not go on with this you've planned."
I rode away to Steierland
and into Graz, a city blessed
by many doctors; one was best.
I went to see him and inquired
if he would do what I desired.

88 He spoke, "Next spring come back again,
sometime in May, I'll cut you then
but not before. Return to me
and on my honor you will see
I'll make your mouth to such a fit
that you'll be really pleased with it.
I'm quite a master at this art
and, what is more, I'm pretty smart."

89 I spent the winter visiting
the ladies all around. When spring
and brighter days were coming on
and winter's ice and snow were gone
and birds were singing on every bough,
I thought, "I must be going now
to Graz and to the doctor's knife.
May God in mercy spare my life!"

90 In Heavens's care I left that day.
I soon encountered on the way
my lady's page, a youth I knew,
who saw and recognized me too.
He said, "Hello," and asked where I
was travelling, then asked me why.
"I'll tell you all about it friend;
it's rather strange what I intend.

91 "You see how well I am and strong,
yet I'll be sick enough ere long
and badly wounded in the head."
The fellow crossed himself and said,
"But, sir, what for, this thing is queer."
I spoke, "My friend, see here, and here.
It looks like three lips, when they're done
with cutting, I'll be missing one."

92 "God help you if it's true," he spoke,
"I quite agree, and do not joke,
it's most surprising, every bit.
My lady hasn't heard of it,
I fancy, and I'll let her know.
You must be mad in acting so,
to take such chances with no need;
why it could cost your life, indeed."

94 He rode his way and I rode mine,
to get to Graz was my design.
I sought and found the doctor there,
at once he took me in his care.
'T was Monday morning, not yet late,
when he began to operate.
He wished me bound but I would not.
He said, "You know, this hurts a lot.

17

95   "And if you move by just a hair
you'll come to harm, so best take care."
I spoke, "You needn't be concerned
for I came freely when I learned
that you could fix this mouth for me.
No matter what the pain may be
no one will ever see me flinch,
not by a fraction of an inch."

96   My fear was not so great at that.
Before him on a bench I sat.
He took the blade and with a slash
he cut into my face a gash.
Down to the teeth his razor went,
which I endured without lament
and, with the surgery complete,
had yet to tremble on my seat.

105   But now I think enough's been said
of how my mouth was cut and bled
to suit my lady. Now I'll tell
you all about what then befell.
My stay at Graz was long extended—
until my face was fully mended.
Then on my way I quickly rode
until I came to my aunt's abode.

106   While she was still far off she spied
my mouth. Now hark to what she cried,
"No one will e'er again decline
you for your mouth. It looks just fine.
I'm really very pleased about
the way your suit is turning out.
The tale already has been told
to me of how you were so bold.

107   "The story will not go to waste.
I wrote the whole thing up in haste
and soon shall send it to the place
where you so bravely seek for grace;
I mean your charming lady fair.
I'll tell her what you did and swear
on all my hope of Heaven's bliss
that she's responsible for this."

109
"May God send rich rewards to you,
my messenger so sweet and true!
Oh aunt, you make me feel so good
and I'd repay you if I could
but you have done so much, I know,
I'll never pay the debt I owe.
I always knew I could rely
on you. But here's a song that I

110
"composed. Please write it carefully
and send it on to her from me.
In Graz while I so long was ill
I worked on it with all my skill.
Her praises turn my grief aside,
her praises fill my heart with pride,
her praises always make me gay,
but hear! The song has this to say:"

THIS IS THE SECOND DANCE TUNE

What shall I sing
about the night? I have no pleasure then.
The day must bring
fulfillment of my hopes—I see again.
Besides, its light
recalls the sight
of her I love, and is a true delight.

Well may he praise
the night who lies with love and shares its bliss,
but it dismays
my lonely heart. I hate the night for this
and praise the day
for then I may
see her who drives my sorrows all away.

I celebrate
the day when first I saw my lady fair.
Since then I wait
for dawn with more and more of grief and care.
The night's to blame
that I became
so sad. But, Day, most blessed be thy name.

I am possessed
at night by grief and hosts of anxious fears.
They're put to rest
at once as soon as day's first light appears.
For then I know
that I must go
and watch in secret her whom I love so.

Oh gladly would
I praise the night if it were not in vain,
or if I could
lie beside the one who brings me pain.
If it might be,
what ecstasy!
Alas, she will not grant this joy to me.

111   "The song and letter I shall send
and to the words already penned
shall add the other things I've learned.
I'll tell her that you've just returned
and see it's clearly understood
that now your mouth looks just as good
as any other man's. Thereby
I'll not be telling her a lie.

112   "The answer which I get from her
I'll send to you, if you prefer,
so you will know what's on her mind."
"Do, aunt, your messenger will find
me at the castle on the Mur."
With this I left her; feeling sure
and happy with this suit of mine,
I took the road to Liechtenstein.

113   My aunt, as soon as I had gone,
took song and note and sent them on
directly to the castle where
her servant found my lady fair.
He didn't have to wait for long;
as soon as she had read the song
and note, she penned a letter such
that, when I got it, pleased me much.

<table>
<tr><td>114</td><td>The letter reached my aunt and she
dispatched it quickly on to me.
The servant didn't spare his horse;
I've her to thank for this, of course.
The letter made my heart so light
and filled my soul with proud delight.
No message ever brought such cheer
to me. But only listen here:</td></tr>
</table>

"My best wishes and my devotion I gladly extend to you and inform you that next Monday I shall leave the castle where I am still residing and shall journey to the castle which you well know, and shall stay overnight at the market which lies near you. Now I beg that you will not fail to visit me there. Then I shall respond to everything which you spoke of in your message. If your nephew wishes to come too I shall be glad to see him—to find out how his mouth looks and for no other reason."

The Adventure of How Sir Ulrich First Spoke With His Lady

<table>
<tr><td>115</td><td>I started when the contents were
made known to me and rode to her,
and I was very happy then
in thoughts of seeing her again.
I came with spirits high, but oh,
the lovely one was guarded so
that evening that I never had
a glimpse of her, which made me sad.</td></tr>
<tr><td>116</td><td>I didn't sleep at all that night
and with the early morning light
got up and went to where I knew
were staying all her retinue.
Knights and many a page were there.
When greeted with a friendly air
at once they answered with respect
and manners cordial and correct.</td></tr>
<tr><td>117</td><td>How quickly did the hour pass!
My lady's chaplain sang a mass
which filled my heart with joy for I
could watch the lady on the sly.
I'd gone with fear to where she met
her guests and I was trembling yet.
She'd bowed to me when she had heard
my greeting, but had said no word.</td></tr>
</table>

119   The mass was over. Speedily
they told the other men and me
to leave the chamber. It was plain
they wouldn't let a man remain.
My lady ate and rode away.
I went to see what aunt would say.
She laughed and tenderly began,
"You surely are a lucky man.

120   "My lady says that she'll permit
you now to come and talk a bit
and say whatever's on your mind;
she's rather favorably inclined.
You'll follow when she starts to ride
and chance to come up by her side;
then you may tell what's on your heart,
but tell it quickly and depart."

121   This made me happy and, of course,
I very soon was on my horse.
When I beheld her up ahead
my heart spoke out with joy and said,
"Now there! Now you at last will speak
with her and tell her what you seek.
She rides before you all alone.
Go up and make your wishes known!"

122   Without delay I hurried there,
but when the lady was aware
of me she turned away her face,
which made me feel quite out of place
and I became so shy therefrom
that tongue and lips at once were dumb.
My head sank down irresolute
and I was silent as a mute.

123   There rode up then another knight
and I dropped back, still dumb with fright.
I rode behind subdued by fear.
This time my heart was more severe,
"You coward, why should you retreat
before a lady who's so sweet,
who wouldn't do you any harm?
Why lose your voice in such alarm?"

130   Again I rode up to her side,
quite pale with fear I could not hide,
my dread of speaking plagued me so.
My heart then gave me many a blow
and leaped within me ever higher,
to talk right out was its desire.
It spoke, "Now speak, now speak, now speak!
She's all alone, don't be so weak!"

131   I opened my mouth ten times at least
to talk. Each time my fear increased.
My tongue was still so tightly bound
I couldn't utter a word or sound.
I'll not discuss this any more;
I left her as I'd done before
and didn't say a single word.
Five times that day the same occurred.

132   There came at last the journey's end.
The lady stopped where she would spend
the night; they'd saved for her a room.
The parting filled my heart with gloom.
I took the stirrup which one needs
to lift the ladies from their steeds
and helped them down with this device.
(Some of them were really nice.)

133   She waited there, the kind and good,
upon her steed. Around her stood
many a knight and page. With these
my lady liked to joke and tease.
I took the stirrup to where she sat;
she spoke, "You've not the strength for that.
You cannot lift me down, for you
are frail and weak, and tired too."

134   Loud was the laughter of the men.
She stepped upon the stirrup then
and from the saddle down she slipped,
but, as I lowered her, she gripped
my hair and, so that none could see,
she quickly tore a lock from me.
"That's what you get for being shy!
What I've been told of you's a lie."

135   She joined her friends when this was said.
                    I stayed behind with lowered head
                    and thought, "What happened to me indeed!
                    I must in honesty concede
                    no one was ever such a dunce;
                    she must have thought that more than once!
                    She'll surely never let me serve
                    her now. I got what I deserve."

136   I lingered on in dark despair.
                    A knight said I should go from there:
                    't was time the ladies got some rest.
                    I rode downtown where I could best
                    secure myself a lodging place.
                    I prayed to God that by His grace
                    He'd take this life which was so sad
                    and all the other things I had.

142   Why should I tell the night's sad tale,
                    of each lament and every wail
                    until the coming of the day?
                    Sometimes I sat, sometimes I lay,
                    sometimes got up and walked about,
                    now in the room and now without.
                    I often wrung my hands with woe;
                    a cousin came and found me so.

143   'T was early yet. Without ado
                    he spoke to me, "What's wrong with you?"
                    I said, "I've got a frightful ache,
                    my heart feels like it soon would break,
                    the pain increases more and more,
                    and that's what I'm so troubled for.
                    I cannot lie nor stand nor sit
                    but walking helps a little bit."

144   "They've got a doctor here," he said.
                    "Bring him to me." Away he sped
                    to find out where the man might be.
                    I had them get a horse for me,
                    a servant too. We then took flight
                    from the hostel where I'd spent the night
                    and raced like a crazy man might run
                    to where I'd left the lovely one.

145   As I approached at breakneck speed
I saw her mounted on her steed
and riding toward me down the street.
'T was just like I had hoped we'd meet.
In handsome dress along she rode
with hooded cape as is the mode.
When she looked up, she made a bow.
I was no longer silent now.

146   I spoke, "My lady, let me find
for love of God that you are kind
to me, and through the nobleness
that God permits you to possess.
Be kind, O lady, full of grace,
may I see favor in your face.
In you do all my joys unite;
you are my feast of pure delight.

147   "You must believe what now you hear,
that I have served you every year
since that sweet hour I'll ne'er forget,
so long ago when first we met.
I'm in your service as your man,
I'll serve you just the best I can
and never anyone but you.
You can be sure that I'll be true.

150   "For you, my lady kind and good,
I'd risk my life whene'er I could
in any knightly deed or game
and always do it in your name.
Whatever way a knight can serve
I'll serve you well, as you deserve.
I should, I will, indeed I must
remain your knight till I am dust."

151   "Silence, you're nothing but a youth,
for these high things still too uncouth.
You'll stop such childish chattering
if my regard is worth a thing
and ride away from me at once.
You still are something of a dunce!
This talk can bring you grief and care
and will not get you anywhere."

152   "It's true, dear lady, I am still
too simple, for I lack the skill
to speak to you the way I ought
or tell my feelings as I sought.
In some respects I'm much more wise
and win from other knights the prize.
I'll serve you thus and shall not fail;
for things like this I'm not too frail."

153   "Just leave me now is my advice,
I shouldn't have to tell you twice.
I don't like talking secretly;
you ought to know they're watching me.
If any knight or lady guessed
what you have said I'd be distressed.
You must be still at once and go!
You're very troublesome, you know."

156   There wasn't any more to say
so I took leave and rode away,
quite pleased. As far as I could tell,
my suit was going rather well.
At least I'd told my ladylove
in part what I'd been thinking of.
My spirits mounted more and more;
I'd never felt such joy before.

157   At once I joined a knightly band.
Where'er they gathered in the land
there I was always seen, and none
could fail to know that I was one.
That summer I had so much luck
that one time in a joust I struck
a worthy knight clear off his steed.
(She thanked me later for this deed.)

158   Of my achievements I'd reveal
much more but think that some might feel
I praised myself a bit too much;
so I'll be still for fear of such.
All summer I was filled with pride,
and as a lady's knight should ride
I rode. If I had some success
't was quite deserved, I must confess.

313   With happy heart I journeyed then
to see my gracious aunt again,
just as a man in love would do.
I got a kindly welcome too.
I said, "I pray that God will grant
rewards, my messenger and aunt,
to you whose friendship cannot fade.
My joy depends upon your aid."

314   "If I can help with your request,
nephew, I'll gladly do my best.
Once more to meet your wish I'll send
a message to your lady friend
and tell her, if this be your will,
at Friesach no one showed more skill
or bravery than you. And I
am sure that this will be no lie."

315   "Dear aunt, you always do me good,
I'll always thank you, as I should.
Please send along this poem here;
I do not have the slightest fear
that she'll not like the words or air
for she's so kindly and so fair
and ever generous with praises.
The song describes her with these phrases:"

THE FOURTH DANCE TUNE

Little birds in forest bowers
sing as one their sweetest lay.
On the meadow pretty flowers
bloom against the light of May.
So now blooms my self-esteem
in the thought of her devotion
which enriches my emotion
as a beggar by a dream.

High the hopes I hold and nourish
in the presence of her charms
that my fortune still may flourish
till I hold her in my arms.
Such desire is all my joy.
Now may God in fullest measure
grant that these, the hopes I treasure,
she I love will not destroy.

May the gentle one I cherish
free of fault or broken vow
never cause this dream to perish
which is all I have for now.
May my pleasure never wane,
may I not in tears awaken,
may I laugh, with courage taken
from the solace I shall gain.

Pleasant thoughts and fond desires,
these are all the joys I sing.
But my love for her requires
little more if I may bring
both into her company
that she willingly may tender
something of her charm and splendor
and be ever kind to me.

Blessed May, your gentle weather
warms the whole world with its kiss.
You and all the world together
bring me not a mite of bliss.
For what pleasure could you give
were the lovely one not near me?
She alone has power to cheer me,
from her solace I must live.

318   I left my aunt ere very long.
She sent the letter and the song
to where the charming lady stayed
and answered thus my plea for aid.
When the messenger appeared
the one whom all so much revered
said, "You are welcome. Tell me how
is your dear lady doing now?"

319   He then replied, "Her health is good
and she conveys, as well she should,
her great devotion here to you,
but she has sent a letter too.
Please read it now and let me go
and God will bless you, this I know.
My lady told me to bestir
myself—the letter came from her."

321   She read the letter, laid it by,
and wrote another in reply.
She gave it to the page: "Now tell
your mistress I am glad she's well,
and give her my regards, and let
her have this message. Don't forget
to tell her frankly that I doubt
the contents of her note throughout."

322   The messenger quite soon returned
and sought his mistress. When she learned
he had a note she sent him on
to Leibnitz; that's where I had gone
to take part in a tournament.
Three hundred knights at this event
strove for honor and for gain;
to some came wealth, to others pain.

323   I warmly greeted him who brought
the message and at once we sought
a private place. He gave me then
the note—so kind my aunt has been!
I thought the letter would impart
that which would please my longing heart;
it took away my joy instead.
Now listen here to what it said:

"This nephew the loftiest praise you give,
perhaps since he's a relative.
But other folks never praised him at all,
which makes your praise seem rather small.
When you're so lavish in your praises
I censure you for empty phrases."

324   I never in my life felt worse
than when he read to me this verse;
the message covered me with shame.
I thought, "I'll have to win the fame
that knightly deeds alone can bring
or I shall soon lose everything:
the life, the goods for which I've striven,
and all besides that God has given."

325   I journeyed far to foreign ground
wherever knightly games were found,
be they in earnest or in fun,
I could be seen at any one.
My body and my wealth I spent
quite willingly, 't was my intent.
To show my lady great respect
my steed and I were richly decked.

327   But now the winter's cold came on,
the forest greenery was gone
and silent was the cheerful chant
of birds. I went to see my aunt
and told her of my grief and pain.
She spoke, "I need to make it plain
that you can't send my page once more
to take your message as before.

328   "She has forbidden me, in truth,
to send her e'er again this youth.
She fears the evil talk of some
and won't permit that he should come.
I'd be so foolish were I still
to act contrary to her will
and send him there, and quite in vain;
for this I'd have to be insane."

332   "Auntie, since your messenger
can ne'er again be sent to her
I'll have to find another who
will go. She shan't forbid me to.
For whether joy or pain prevail
my loyalty will never fail.
My heart has thought the whole thing out;
of this there'll never be a doubt.

333 "Aunt, for what you've done for me
I'm just as thankful as can be.
I'll always feel a debt to you;
you may be sure that this is true."
I said goodbye and went along
and, while I rode, composed a song,
quite as my loving heart advised,
about the lady whom I prized.

THE FIFTH DANCE TUNE

Summer now is gone away,
the birds will sing no more this year.
I am left forlorn today:
my heart's sad song alone I hear.
Winter and another grief
together give my heart much pain:
the two conspire against my heart's relief.

Summer's joys do well prepare
the lover's spirit (this I know)
for the service of the fair—
Oh blest be summer's lovely glow!
Hateful winter I despise,
but summer's bliss I love, for then
can one serve well the lady he does prize.

What does winter mean to me,
what good are long, cold winter nights?
Indifferent to this is she
who could grant me such delights.
Would that my distress might end
in the same sweet repose as his
who lies within the arms of his sweet friend.

Sorrow follows love fulfilled:
so should rejoicing follow pain.
Since my sorrow is not stilled,
therefore my hopes all green remain.
Lady, you could change my state
from sadness into greatest joy.
While others dance, my woe does not abate.

Lady dear, oh lady mine,
why do you hate and wound me so?
Service is my sole design,
as you (and God as well) do know.
Never have I gone astray
or let my heart to others turn
since narrow path I knew from crooked way.

334 I rode that winter up and down
to visit ladies near the town
by which she dwelt. I was, I own,
more constant than a precious stone.
My faithful heart considered much
how I might find a servant such
that I could send her, just to tell
how I desired to serve her well.

335 Unhappily the proper kind
of messenger I could not find.
I searched the country end to end
and found not one whom I could send.
This caused my longing heart to grieve
with sorrow nothing could relieve;
my life was nearly empty of
all joy because of thwarted love.

336 Delight was almost gone, but then
the merry summer came again
and brought its charm, as is its way,
and many a beautiful summer day.
I thought, "I'll serve my lady dear
most gladly through another year
and better than I have before,
and so perhaps I'll please her more."

337 No time was wasted, I confess,
till I had steeds and battle dress.
I'd soon forsaken my abode,
to Carinthia and Krain I rode
and down to Istria. 'T was there
that Meinhart von Gorze bade them prepare
Triest for many a knightly game,
which served to further spread his fame.

338　Before the knightly sport was done
　　a name for many a man was won
　　who so excelled in knightly arts
　　that he subdued the ladies' hearts.
　　Count Meinhart jousted very well,
　　as oft before and since befell.
　　I know at least a hundred spears
　　were broken there by cavaliers.

339　I used up fifteen spears with skill
　　and bravery. I stayed until
　　the games were over. Then I went
　　to Brixen to a tournament.
　　My dress was courtly as can be,
　　my only thought was chivalry.
　　I wished to serve my lady sweet
　　with many a bold and daring feat.

The Adventure of How Sir Ulrich Lost His Finger

340　When I arrived there many a knight
　　received me warmly, as was right;
　　their courtly manners were the best.
　　They knew how one receives a guest
　　and greeted me with such display
　　that I felt welcome right away,
　　for one could tell they wished to please.
　　I thanked them all and felt at ease.

341　The sides were chosen for the game
　　and with the morning light we came
　　onto the Merre, a nearby field;
　　we hurried there with spear and shield.
　　It soon began; so I was told,
　　a hundred valiant knights and bold
　　strove with each other up and down
　　the field that day and won renown.

342   At last it was empty of steeds and men
but only hear what happened then.
Sir Ulschalk von Bozen challenged me
to show my lady constancy
and break with him a spear or two;
this I was very glad to do.
Before another word was said
each tied his helmet on his head.

343   With heavy lances poised in air
we charged upon each other there;
the joust was finely executed.
Sir Ulschalk, who is well reputed,
struck my hand while passing by
and knocked a finger off, so I
had to remove my helmet then
to show I couldn't joust again.

345   We rode at once to town to find
a doctor who would come and bind
my hand. Soon one was at my side.
He saw the wound was deep and wide
but thought the hand could be restored
(the finger hung by a single cord)
He said, "If treated right, I feel
that hand and finger both will heal."

346   These tidings filled my heart with cheer.
I told the doctor, "Listen here,
if what you say to me is true
I'll willingly present to you
more wealth than you will ever need,
enough to make you glad indeed.
Just save the finger and you'll get
a thousand pounds to pay my debt."

347   At once the doctor took command.
He carefully tied up my hand
and in the bandages it lay
right up to the seventh day.
But, when the doctor then unbound
the hand to see the wound, he found
that it was swollen and so black
that even he was taken aback.

350 My heart was filled with deep dismay.
A worthy doctor, I'd heard say,
was near, at Bozen, so I spurred
my horse and left for I had heard,
if I should come before too late,
the doctor's learning was so great
that he would surely save my finger.
I rode to him and did not linger.

352 I entered Bozen then in haste.
The doctor also did not waste
much time but came to do my will;
I'd sent him word that I was ill.
He saw my wound, examined it,
and said, "You need not fret a bit.
It won't take long for me to cure
your hand and finger, I am sure."

373 I sought a messenger whom I
could send. I'll tell you, it's no lie,
there simply wasn't one to find,
which quite disturbed my peace of mind.
I couldn't even let her know
that all for her I suffered so.
This worried me; the truth to tell,
I didn't like it very well.

374 My thoughts were troubled, but in vain;
my finger also caused me pain.
The wound was often bound for me
which made it bleed quite heavily.
Twice daily I endured this curse
but still my spirit pained me worse.
To find no person to employ
as messenger killed every joy.

375 A messenger at any cost
I had to have or all was lost;
with great concern my heart was stirred.
But listen now to what occurred:
Not far away there lived a youth,
my friend, and one who spoke the truth.
He came to see me and express
his sympathy in my distress.

376   "God knows I wouldn't say to you,"
he spoke, "a thing that wasn't true;
I pledge my hope of Heaven's bliss
that I am worried over this.
If I could have my way, I know
I'd gladly take on me your woe
and every pain I'd gladly bear.
I'd do it, on my word I swear."

377   I spoke, "I do not doubt you would
and I believe you, as I should;
you've been a friend. My heart will break
with sorrow more than it can take
in thinking of a lady sweet
whom I have served with many a feat.
Could I but find a messenger
to say I got this wound for her!"

378   "Sir Friend, hear this I have to say:
it's not two weeks ago today
since I have seen your lady fair.
If I may do so, I declare
that I have known her just the same
although you never spoke her name.
I know her well enough to state
that you're no object of her hate."

386   I spoke, "It's well that you're my friend.
That I've done nothing to offend
you, I am very glad to hear,
especially since you are dear
to her. That you can tell her what
you wish, this cheers my heart a lot.
For you, my friend, will have to be
the messenger to her from me."

387   "I'll be the messenger you need
and carry any news indeed
which you may want her to receive.
That I'll do this you must believe.
I'll quickly tell her what you will
and bring the answer, good or ill,
to you at once. I'll not suppress
a thing, though it be 'No' or 'Yes.' "

388   "Friend, I pray that God requite
your help to me in this sad plight.
Now tell the lady from us both
and swear to her a solemn oath
that I have always loved her best,
more than myself and all the rest,
and also more than any thing.
I serve her with no wavering.

389   "You ought to let the lady know
that only several days ago
I lost a finger which was born
to serve her. This I've often sworn.
'T was in a joust. I'll not complain
but gladly suffer loss or gain
for her, and never seek relief
from either happiness or grief.

390   "Now ask the lady if she'll let
me be her knight, and don't forget
to beg her by the charm in which
God in his kindness made her rich
that she will send me cheerful news
to end the sorrow that subdues
my heart. You ought to talk about
these things with her. Leave nothing out."

392   He said goodbye and then he rode
until he came to her abode.
When he arrived my lady fair
at once bade him be welcome there.
She said, "Friend, you must tell me how
your mistress is; what's she doing now?
Be sure you tell me just the truth
and only that, well-mannered youth."

393   The page's answer was refined:
"Gracious lady fair and kind,
since it's the truth that you prefer,
well then, I haven't come from her.
A knight has sent me here, I own,
whose sore distress I long have known.
He sends you, lady good and pure,
a loyalty which will endure.

394

"He bade me tell you his distress
and hopes you'll grant his suit success.
Quite recently he was so true
that he was wounded serving you.
I ought to tell you what it cost:
a finger from his hand was lost.
He used it just to serve you right
and lost it as a gallant knight.

395

"He's chosen you, is what he swore,
to be his lady evermore,
and with such constant loyalty
that he will ne'er be sorrow free
unless you're favorably inclined
to him, my lady good and kind.
You're more than all the world to him,
than riches, ladies, life and limb."

396

"Tell me who has been so bold
and sent the message you have told.
God knows that I don't care for it.
What man could have so little wit
to send you here with such a claim?
Speak up! I'd like to learn his name.
And you should know that you don't please
me when you bring me words like these."

397

"Lady, the name I'll gladly tell
for he has always kept it well.
He's called The Knight of Liechtenstein,
Sir Ulrich; he's a friend of mine
whom you can trust, and I am sure
that his devotion will endure;
he's never won so great a prize
as you, dear lady fair and wise.

398

"My lady sweet, if you would yield
and let him be a while concealed
alone with you 't would be such bliss.
He'd not exchange the Grail for this
which valiant Parzifal did gain
with knightly deeds and bitter pain.
His heaven and his paradise
is you, so lovely and so nice."

399   "Tell him from me, you courtly boy,
      I'll not permit him to destroy
      my peace this way. He must console
      himself and find another goal
      more suitable to him, for I
      shall certainly grow old and die
      and all the while learn nothing of
      that which is known as secret love.

405   "Here's the message you're to bring
      (take care and don't forget a thing):
      he'll quit the service he's begun
      or lose the honor he has won.
      If he believes my mind will change
      he'll quickly find that I'll arrange
      that he shall suffer such disgrace
      he'll never want to show his face."

407   "I'll tell him, lady, as I should,
      though it will surely do no good.
      His mind is fixed, dear lady, so
      that he'll not let his service go.
      He can't be stopped by pain or need
      or even fear of death, indeed,
      and will not leave your service now
      no matter what may come, I vow."

408   He said goodbye and then returned
      to where I waited, quite concerned.
      I saw the messenger come near
      and what I said you now shall hear,
      "Be welcomed by both God and me,
      you page, so skilled in courtesy.
      Tell me, were you successful there?
      How did you leave my lady fair?"

409   "She is healthy, she is gay.
      She instructed me to say.
      you'll leave her service without ado
      if life and honor are dear to you.
      Should you not heed the words she sends,
      through other means she'll gain her ends
      and bring such mischief on your head
      that you'll be overcome with dread."

411   "My friend, no matter what may come,
no matter what I suffer from,
my service shall continue on
until my life itself is gone.
Though things go well, though things go ill,
't is she I'll serve, such is my will,
and while I live no joy shall stir
my heart but that which comes from her."

419   I spent the summer in Steierland
and often tied my helmet band.
To earn my lady's love I meant
to joust with knights where'er I went,
and very eagerly I fought.
With constant faithfulness I sought
to serve her as a suitor should
who hopes that his reward is good.

420   The summer and every summer joy
were gone. Once more I urged the boy
(I mean the messenger) that he
would see the lady fair for me.
He spoke, "To her I'll gladly ride
and tell whatever you confide,
of how you sorrow and you pine,
and speak as if the thoughts were mine."

421   I told to him without delay
just what I wanted him to say
and sent to her a song again.
With joy he parted from me then.
When he had reached her dwelling place
she welcomed him with friendly grace.
"Pardon," he said, "if I intrude,
I hope you're in a better mood

422   "than you were in when last we met."
The lady answered with regret,
"What have I done to cause offense?
Now tell me that without pretense.
You know, you always have been dear
to me. You can be happy here,
and though I may not always please
you never need feel ill at ease."

423   "God pay you from his boundless store!
I come as messenger once more
to bring a message from a knight
who seeks for favor in your sight
and offers, lady dear, to you
a greeting and his service too,
esteem and loyalty and love,
and all a man is master of."

430   "You're both quite good at flattering
but I shall tell you this one thing:
you said (it really makes me mad),
in serving me Sir Ulrich had
lost a finger. I deny
the boast and think it just a lie.
I'm told, he has the finger still.
I wish you wouldn't do his will."

431   "Lady, he has it, I'll admit,
and yet, so badly bent is it,
it cannot do him any good
and doesn't help him as it should
for he can't move it very well.
But one thing I'll be glad to tell:
it firmly holds, so it appears,
in serving you some heavy spears."

432   "I'm glad his finger's on his hand
but lies as this I cannot stand.
He has it still, and you have told
a lie in part; that's why I scold.
Now I shall talk with you no more,
so go back where you were before
and, courtly boy, you'd better see
you bring no messages to me."

433   My messenger departed then
and soon was back with me again.
When I caught sight of him I cried,
"Dear messenger, come right inside
and tell what happened right away.
What did the lovely lady say?
If I should hear good news at last
my heart will never be downcast."

434   "She didn't send a word to you
but she told me a thing or two.
I'm not to be your messenger;
she said, it greatly vexes her
and gives her cause to be irate
that I should come to her and state,
you lost a finger and were maimed
for her. It was a lie, she claimed.

435   "She heard the finger was all right
and she believes the wound was slight;
what I have told of you is lies
and I've deceived her, she implies.
She's peeved at me and quite upset
but glad you have the finger yet.
She wouldn't have the wound be bad,
it's just the lie that makes her mad."

436   I thought, "Because my lady dear
is vexed about this finger here,
that I still have it, 't would be best
(since it's less useful than the rest)
to cut it off and have him leave
the thing with her. For she'll believe
it's really lost when she looks at
it then. It goes, and that is that."

437   I left him and at once began
to seek a certain honest man,
von Hasendorf, so he was named,
Sir Ulrich, who was widely famed
for courage and a level head.
He wished to serve me, so he said.
I bade him show his loyalty
and cut a finger off for me.

440   "I'll do your will, you may depend
on me for truly I'm your friend,
and vassal too. I wish to serve
you always, as you well deserve."
I took his knife and unafraid
across my finger set the blade.
I spoke, "Now strike, good man, and well!"
He struck, and from my hand it fell.

441   While still the blood was running strong
        my well-bred courier came along
        and quickly whispered in my ear,
        "What now? What are you doing here?
        Did you cut off your finger? Oh,
        for this my heart condemns me so
        because of what I've seen and heard
        and that I told you a single word."

442   "My friend, you needn't start a row,
        just take to her my finger now
        and tell her that she can depend
        on this: I'll serve her to the end
        with loyalty that's never swayed.
        And if this service is not paid—
        that, of all women everywhere,
        I've chosen her—it won't be fair."

443   "It grieves me so to see you bleed
        but now that you have done the deed
        you should compose a note of praise
        with many a pretty word and phrase
        to send, whatever else you do.
        Of course I'll take the finger too.
        I'm pleased to help in your distress;
        God grant my trip complete success."

444   "I'll gladly do it since I can."
        At once I started and began
        a very nice and clever lay.
        With it my finger rode away
        to where the lady dear was seen.
        In velvet, soft and grassy green,
        they wound the verses speedily.
        I had a goldsmith make for me

445   without delay two bands of gold.
        In these the lay was put. To hold
        it firm was made a little clasp
        in shape like tiny hands that grasp
        each other—all was formed with care.
        The finger now was put in there.
        When everything would satisfy
        the messenger then said goodbye.

446   I spoke, "God care for you, I pray,
while there as well as on the way!"
With this, I watched the page depart
and stayed behind with heavy heart.
The verse was hidden in his coat
when he arrived, so none took note.
He went to her with fear and dread;
the lady looked at him and said,

447   "I welcome you again, young squire,
although you really stirred my ire.
If you have something new to tell
I'll let you speak. What now befell?"
"Dear lady," quickly spoke the boy,
"my lord has chosen to employ
me once again, and to entrust
me with the finger we discussed."

448   He showed her then the little book
which the lovely lady took,
and you'll believe her great surprise
when the finger met her eyes.
"Alas," she said, "what have you brought?
I'm sure I never would have thought
that any person sound of mind
could be so foolish or so blind."

450   She read my verses to the end
and spoke at once, "My youthful friend,
what can I tell you? I'll not hide
my sorrow that the finger died
but that's not fondness for the knight.
I'm sad because you may be right
in saying that it thus was slain
because of me. This gives me pain."

451   "Lady, I'll tell you how it went.
Not long ago when I was sent
away from here he then received
the news that you were very peeved
at me for saying, lady grand,
he'd lost a finger from his hand
in knightly service, and that you
were mad because it wasn't true.

452 "He left me quickly when he heard
the story. Lady, take my word
that almost on the very spot
he found a vassal whom he got
to cut his finger off and maim
him thus. Right after that I came
and when I saw him bleeding still,
I must confess, it made me ill."

453 "Go back and tell him my regret;
he'd serve the ladies better yet,
were it not that his hand is shy
a finger. Tell him too that I
shall always keep the finger near,
buried in my dresser here,
that I shall see it every day,
and that I mean just what I say.

454 "Tell him from me now, courtly youth:
I'll keep the finger—not, in truth,
because my heart at last is moved
so that his prospects are improved
by a single hair. Make sure he hears
this: should he serve a thousand years,
the service I would always scorn.
By my constancy I've sworn."

455 With this the messenger returned.
When he recounted all he'd learned
I was pleased with the whole affair;
that she had kept the finger there
was enough to fill my heart with joy
and so I said this to the boy,
"I'm very glad to hear that she
will keep the finger there for me.

456 "Whene'er she sees it, this is plain,
she cannot possibly refrain
from thinking that I serve her well.
She has it and her mind will dwell
on me. The prospect does me good.
I'll serve her always as I should,
on her my pleasures all depend,
she is my May and winter's end.

458   "My service must be God's command.
Now let me tell you what I've planned.
I'll take on woman's dress and name
and thus disguised will strive for fame.
Sweet God protect me and sustain!
I'll travel with a knightly train
up to Bohemia from the sea.
A host of knights shall fight with me.

459   "This very winter I shall steal
out of the land and shall conceal
my goal from everyone but you.
I'll travel as a pilgrim who
to honor God is bound for Rome
(no one will question this at home).
I'll stop in Venice and shall stay
in hiding till the first of May.

460   "I'll carefully remain unseen
but deck myself out like a queen;
it should be easy to acquire
some lovely feminine attire
which I'll put on—now hear this last—
and when St. George's day is past,
the morning afterwards, I'll ride
(I pray that God is on my side)

461   "from the sea to Mestre, near
by Venice. He who breaks a spear
with me to serve, by tourneying,
his lady fair will get a ring
of gold and it will be quite nice.
I'll give it to him with this advice,
that he present it to his love,
the one he's in the service of.

463   "Messenger, I'll make the trip
so there will never be a slip
and no one possibly can guess
whose form is hid beneath the dress.
For I'll be clad from head to toe
in woman's garb where'er I go,
fully concealed from people's eyes.
They'll see me only in disguise.

465   "If you would please me, messenger,
then travel once again to her.
Just tell her what I have in mind
and ask if she will be so kind
as to permit that I should fight
throughout this journey as her knight.
It's something she will not repent
and I'll be glad of her assent."

466   He rode at once to tell her this
and swore upon his hope of bliss
my loyalty would never falter,
that I was true and would not alter.
He told my plan in full detail
and said, "My lady, should you fail
to let him serve and show your trust
in him, it wouldn't seem quite just."

467   "Messenger," she spoke, "just let
him have this message, don't forget.
This trip, if I have understood
you right, will surely do him good
and he will win a rich reward
in praise from many a lady and lord.
Whether it helps with me or not,
from others he will gain a lot."

468   The messenger was pleased and sure.
He found me by the river Mur
at Liechtenstein where I was then.
'T was nice to have him there again.
I spoke, "O courtly youth, now tell
me if the lady's feeling well.
For, if my darling's doing fine,
then shall rejoice this heart of mine."

469   He spoke, "She's fair and happy too;
she bade me bring this word to you
about your journey. If you should
go through with it 't will do you good
and, whether it helps with her or not,
from others you will gain a lot.
She certainly supports your aim
and says that you'll be rich in fame.

47

The Adventure of How Sir Ulrich, Dressed as a Queen, Rode Tourneying
Through the Lands

470   I listened to the news he had,
and heart and body both were glad.
It was a joy for me to know
my undertaking pleased her so.
I didn't linger but began
at once to carry out my plan
and was quite happy, I admit,
that he also approved of it.

471   I soon was ready, I assure
you, to begin my knightly tour.
I started out as pilgrim dressed
and left the land. I thought it best
to take a staff and pouch at least,
for looks (I got them from a priest);
one would have thought me bound for Rome.
I prayed God bring me safely home.

472   I got to Venice without delay
and found a house in which to stay,
right on the edge of town, a place
where none would ever see my face
who might have recognized me there.
I was as cautious everywhere
and all the winter long I hid.
But let me tell you what I did:

473   I had some woman's clothing made
to wear throughout the masquerade.
They cut and sewed for me twelve skirts
and thirty fancy lady's shirts.
I bought two braids for my disguise,
the prettiest they could devise,
and wound them with some pearls I got
which didn't cost an awful lot.

474
I bade the tailors then prepare
three velvet cloaks for me to wear,
all white. The saddles too on which
the master labored, stitch by stitch,
were silver white. As for a king
was made the saddle covering,
long and broad and gleaming white.
The bridles all were rich and bright.

475
The tailors sewed for every squire
(there were a dozen) white attire.
A hundred spears were made for me
and all as white as they could be.
But I need not continue so,
for all I wore was white as snow
and everything the squires had on
was just as white as any swan.

476
My shield was white, the helmet too.
I had them make ere they were through
a velvet cover for each steed
as armor. These were white, indeed,
as was the battle cape which I
should wear for jousting by and by,
the cloth of which was very fine.
I was quite pleased to call it mine.

477
At last I had my horses sent
to me (none knew just where they went)
and got some servants, as I'd planned,
each native to a foreign land.
They carefully did not let slip
a thing about my coming trip
and I took heed that those who came
to serve me never learned my name.

478
Soon we were all prepared to go;
how pleased was I that this was so.
I sent a letter on apace
by messenger to every place
where I had planned to stop awhile
and urged upon him craft and guile
that none might ever guess or hear
my name. He said I needn't fear.

479   In the message I composed
my journey was in full disclosed:
each hostel where I would alight
to eat and drink and spend the night,
and all that one might wish to learn.
Before the messenger's return
indeed a month at least had sped.
Now this is what the letter said:

"The noble Queen Venus, Goddess of Love, sends to all of the knights who reside in Lombardy, Friuli, Carinthia, Styria, Austria, and Bohemia her good wishes and her greeting and announces that, because of her love, she will journey to them and will teach them with what sort of things they should earn or win the love of noble ladies. She announces to them that the day after Saint George's Day she will rise from the sea at Mestre and will travel as far as Bohemia on this mission. Whichever knight comes against her and breaks a spear in two against her she will reward with a golden ring which he is to send to the lady whom he loves most. The ring has the power to make the lady to whom it is sent all the more beautiful and to cause her to love faithfully him who sent it to her. If my Lady Venus unhorses a knight, he is to bow toward the four ends of the world in honor of a woman. If she however, is unhorsed by a knight, he is to have all of the horses which she brings with her. She will ride the first day to Treviso, the next day to the Piave River, the third day to Sacile, the fourth day to St. Odorico, the fifth day to Gemona, the sixth day to Chiusa Pass, the seventh day to Tarvisio, the eighth day to Villach. She will spend the ninth day there quietly. The tenth day to Feldkirchen, the eleventh day to St. Veith, the twelfth day to Friesach, the thirteenth day to Scheifling, the fourteenth day to Judenburg, the fifteenth day to Knittelfeld, the sixteenth day to Leoben, the seventeenth day to Kapfenberg, the eighteenth day to Mürzzuschlag, the nineteenth day to Gloggnitz. She will remain there for the twentieth day. On the twenty-first day she will be in Neunkirchen, on the twenty-second day she will be at Neustadt, on the twenty-third day she will be at Traiskirchen, on the twenty-fourth day she will be at Vienna where she will remain over the twenty-fifth day, on the twenty-sixth day she will be at Korneuburg, on the twenty-seventh day she will be at Mistelbach, on the twenty-eighth day she will be at Feldsberg, on the twenty-ninth day she will be beyond the Thaya River in Bohemia; there her journey will end. On the journey she will let no one see either her face or her hands; she will also not say a word to anyone. She decrees that on the eighth day after the end of her journey there shall be a tournament at Korneuburg. Whichever knight hears of her journey and does not come against her she places under the ban of love and of all good women. She has listed all of her stopping places that each knight may know where or when he may come against her, so that it may be most convenient for him."

480   Where'er this document was shown
or read to make my journey known
it made a lot of happy men.
In German lands the custom then
was such that none had honored names
who did not strive in knightly games
or win through ladies joy and pride.
I wish this custom had not died.

481   Each knight prepared with joyful heart
to welcome me. 'T was time to start;
now that Saint Georges's Day was past
my journey could begin at last.
'T was early when I started out
but soon the people thronged about
and many walked along behind.
Great feats of valor filled my mind.

482   My marshal and my cook, with three
to help them, led the company;
they cared for food and bed and more.
Behind them came a man who bore
a banner, white as any swan;
two rode beside him, playing on
their horns. They made so loud a sound
that Mestre echoed round and round.

483   My three pack horses then were led
along, a groom at each one's head—
good lads and fit for any deeds.
There followed them three battle steeds,
each with its groom that it not lack
for care, and on each horse's back
was fixed a saddle, silver white.
The saddler knew his trade all right.

484   Beside a battle steed was born
my shield of white. I would have sworn
a finer one I'd never seen
nor one as suited for a queen.
My helmet too was carried there;
none shone like this one anywhere.
On top of it a crown was wrought
which was quite splendid, so I thought.

485   A flutist was the next to come
       who beat with skill upon a drum.
       Four squires were riding after him
       in uniforms of modish trim
       and each had brought three spears along,
       well-made and large, which with a thong
       were bound together. One could praise
       these bearers for their courtly ways.

486   Two maidens rode behind the squires
       and every bit of their attires
       was gleaming white from head to toe.
       They both looked very pretty so.
       A fiddler rode behind each maid;
       my heart was happy when they played,
       and when the two would fiddle high
       a marching tune most pleased was I.

487   I followed after all the rest,
       in shining raiment richly dressed.
       My cloak was velvet and was white
       as was my hat, but this was bright
       with many pearls on every side.
       My loving heart was filled with pride
       that I should serve my lady now
       with knightly deeds and keep my vow.

488   The braids I had were thick and brown
       and were so long that they hung down
       below my sash, just like a girl's.
       They too were richly decked with pearls
       and in a most artistic way.
       My heart has seldom been so gay.
       Nobody ever owned before
       a fairer skirt than that I wore.

489   I had a white and glossy shirt
       which was as long as was the skirt
       with woman's sleeves of quality
       that made me proud as I could be.
       My gloves were silk and finely made.
       Attired like this and unafraid
       I left the sea as I had vowed,
       and soon collected quite a crowd.

490   They'd only come to look at us.
I had a servant question thus,
"Are there no jousters hereabout?"
They answered, "Lady, yes. No doubt
there are at least a thousand here
who would most gladly break a spear
with you but jousting in this state
is outlawed by the magistrate.

491   "The Lord of Treviso has decreed
that anyone who doesn't heed
and jousts with you upon these grounds
must pay at least five thousand pounds.
We're greatly troubled by this ban.
He's such a grim, forbidding man
and never stops to play awhile.
One almost never sees him smile."

492   I journeyed forth without delay,
dressed in a woman's fine array,
on to Treviso merrily.
A famous count rode up to me
with fifty well-clad mounted men.
We quickly recognized him then
and he was greeted as he came.
Count Meinhart von Gorze was his name.

493   The worthy noble was concerned
when he found out what we had learned:
that we could do no jousting there.
He said, "How's that? Why, who would care?"
"The magistrate," a squire replied.
"It's wrong that this should be denied,"
spoke he, "and knightly games be banned.
Can't we have pleasure in this land?"

494   "I'll go and see why," said the count.
At once he sprang upon his mount
and with his fifty knights behind
him quickly rode away to find
the magistrate. When this was done
he spoke, "Sir, we would have some fun
and this with your permission too.
I ask this favor now of you,"

495   He said, "I gladly shall permit
such fun as brings no harm with it;
of joy I'm really not a foe.
But here is something you must know.
I certainly shall not allow
a knight into Treviso now
with armor on and spear in hand.
This is denied by my command.

496   "Too many strangers journey here;
that's why I need to be severe
and make each knight obey this rule.
In truth, I'd really be a fool
were I to let these people arm.
It easily could bring us harm;
so who would joust must travel thence.
Of course, I mean you no offense."

497   With this he left the magistrate
and in a rage he hurried straight
to where he found the womenfolk
and of his grievance quickly spoke,
"You fair and noble ladies sweet,
by all your virtues I entreat
that you will hear as I complain.
The magistrate bade us refrain

498   "from jousting further in this place.
No knight has suffered such disgrace
here in Treviso e'er before.
He'll not allow it, so he swore,
that anyone of us should arm.
He fears the town will come to harm
and says he has commanded thus
since many strangers come to us."

499   The women spoke without delay,
"He ought to take the ban away.
We'll send and ask him to come by
and do not think he'll then deny
us women such a small request.
When we present it in our best
and sweetest manner he'll consent
to what will make us all content."

500 A courier rode away to seek
him out and say they wished to speak
with him. 'T was then I came inside
the city. People watched me ride
with music playing as we passed
(I'd told them not to go too fast).
With happy heart I entered there,
greeted by many a lady fair.

501 I could not help my feeling proud
surrounded by so great a crowd,
but we got to the inn all right
in which I planned to spend the night.
The magistrate arrived meanwhile
among the ladies. With a smile
each warmly welcomed him and said
a greeting with her lips so red.

502 He bowed as does a courtly man.
The pretty ladies then began
to speak, "You ought to grant us, sire,
the favor which we all desire.
We hope you'll let the queen fulfill
her quest and tourney if she will;
we want to see some lances break.
You should permit it for our sake."

503 "I can't refuse you, it appears,
I'll let Count Meinhart break two spears,
since all you ladies so incline.
Sir Leutfried, Lord of Eppenstein,
at once stepped forward from his place
to ask of him with courtly grace
that he receive this favor too.
The women spoke, "Grant it, lord, do!"

504 "I shall," he said, "but only one.
There'll be no more when this is done."
The count meanwhile with joy had gone
to get his armor quickly on.
His trappings all were very nice
and must have cost the highest price;
his clothing was the very best.
I'll tell you how this knight was dressed.

505   His helmet shone with gold, and it
was hard as diamond, every bit.
A crest of feathers on the crown,
though thick, was almost weighted down
with wealth. The feathers' tops were trimmed
and all the crest was decked and rimmed
with silver leaflets which with skill
were tightly bound to every quill.

508   The cape worn over his cuirass
was velvet and as green as grass.
The saddle cover too was green
and everywhere on both were seen
the coat of arms which decked his shield.
The heavy spears that he could wield
so cleverly were like the clover,
his cape, and saddle—green all over.

509   He had a buckle and a sash
and both would brightly gleam and flash;
his collar and his hose were good
and sparkled just as iron should
whenever it's been rightly wrought.
The gallant noble feared for nought.
He wore two spurs of shining gold.
Thus was attired this knight so bold.

510   The noble Meinhart rode along
upon a charger, swift and strong,
that leaped and bounded as it came.
I heard a lot of folks exclaim
with anxious cries, "Get back, watch out!"
The rider, though, was brave and stout
and had a very knightly air.
The ladies begged him to beware.

511   I too was ready and was bright
in my battle dress of white.
The helmet which I wore was crowned
and sent a glitter all around.
My braids were very long and hung
down to the saddle where they swung.
A net of pearls enclosed each tress,
but one could see them none the less.

514   I thus came riding like a queen
with woman's clothes and knightly mien.
So many folks were in the street
my horse could hardly move his feet.
Whate'er Treviso's ruler said,
although he ordered and he pled
that they would clear for us a ring,
his scolding didn't change a thing.

515   I tell the truth when I declare
so many folks were gathered there
there wasn't any open space
in all Treviso, not a place
where we could joust or that allowed
our steeds to gallop through the crowd.
We met upon a bridge at last
but even there were people massed.

516   Beneath the bridge a river ran.
The magistrate at once began
to drive the people off. He gained
his object; only few remained
and we prepared to joust right here.
The pretty ladies who were near
said prayers that there would be no slips.
These came from many rose-red lips.

517   When I beheld him start his course
without delay I spurred my horse.
He did the same, and so we two
were hurled together, this is true,
as if our horses now could fly.
Each hand was steady, and each eye;
the spears both struck with practiced art
right where the shield and helmet part.

518   The lances made a crashing sound
and splinters flew for yards around;
his shield struck mine, we came so near.
At once each got another spear.
Again we jousted, hard and well,
and so that neither of us fell.
I and this nobleman so bold
broke skilfully six spears, all told.

519 This done, Count Meinhart, good and brave,
untied his helmet. Then I gave
to him a little golden ring,
a gift he was supposed to bring
the lady whom he loved the best
and in so doing manifest
his loyalty and constant mind.
No better token could one find.

520 Sir Leutfried, Lord of Eppenstein,
prepared to joust. His clothes were fine
and all his trappings, every stitch.
The sturdy man was very rich
and known throughout the Mur's high land.
The spear he carried in his hand
was heavy and was painted red,
to show his valor, it was said.

521 I thought, "He's heavy and robust
and certainly knows how to joust."
I took a long approach, for speed;
his spear dropped down too low indeed
and struck my horse's neck. My spear
was shattered on his chest. In fear
and pain my wounded horse sprang high
and quickly on the ground was I.

522 By then the day was almost past.
The jousting had to end at last,
and so I hastened to the inn.
The knights would all have liked to win
a better chance to look at me
but I could never let this be.
I hid from everybody's eyes
throughout the trip, save in disguise.

524 The morning after, when the day
was well advanced (though I still lay
upon my bed) outside the door
two hundred women, maybe more,
had gathered and they wished to know
at what time I had planned to go
to church; and, while they waited, some
began to ask when I would come.

526   As soon as I became aware
       that all these women waited there,
       I dressed myself in clothes so good
       that any noblewomen would
       be glad to wear, and this is true.
       What they were like I'll tell to you:
       I put a shirt on, gleaming white
       and rather long, just as was right,

527   and after that a pair of sleeves;
       no one who's looked at them believes
       that he's seen others just as nice
       or prettier at any price.
       A lovely skirt I then put on
       which was as white as any swan.
       I'm sure no lady ever had
       a better one, and that's not bad.

530   A heavy veil concealed my face
       for I took care that not a trace
       of me should show and none should spy
       more than the glimmer of an eye.
       Thus like a woman I was dressed
       and all I had was of the best.
       The peacock feathers on my hat
       were rather dear, I'll tell you that.

531   I had a glove on either hand,
       the best that money could command.
       I left the room lightheartedly
       and rosy lips then greeted me
       of one accord when I was seen
       with "Welcome Venus, welcome queen!"
       Many were held in high repute
       and some of them were really cute.

532   Before we'd gotten on our way
       Count Meinhart started in to play
       at knightly games. A tournament
       began and knightly riders went
       careering past us on their steeds
       to show us ladies valiant deeds.
       The struggle moved from place to place,
       now here, now there, at furious pace.

533   You must believe that this is so:
        At least five hundred knights, I know,
        were tourneying upon the field.
        One heard the clash of many a shield
        and heard the breaking lances' crash
        and saw there many a rider dash
        into the middle of the strife
        for a ladylove to risk his life.

534   I asked the knights that they arrest
        the game. They honored my request;
        so we went on to church at last.
        A countess held my mantle fast
        and sometimes lifted up my skirt
        that they not draggle in the dirt.
        Like this she led me to the pew;
        I took her service as my due.

536   A priest then sang a pretty mass.
        The crowd was such I could not pass
        to go and give my offering.
        They asked the ladies not to cling
        so close and let me out and in.
        I tripped along so feminine
        they laughed—the women and the men.
        The kiss of peace was started then.

537   I got the peace kiss from a book
        but through my veil, which didn't look
        quite right. I wished to pass the kiss
        on to the countess; she said this:
        "You'll have to move the veil aside
        for such a kiss I can't abide."
        When she spoke thus I did not quail
        but from my lips drew back the veil.

538   The charming lady then began
        to laugh and said, "Why you're a man!
        I caught a glimpse of you just now.
        What then? I'll kiss you anyhow.
        From all good women everywhere
        I'll give a kiss. Because you wear
        a woman's dress and honor thus
        us all, I'll kiss for all of us."

539   When she spoke up so merrily
and took the kiss of peace from me
my heart and mind were filled with bliss
for joy is but a lady's kiss.
I'm sure that everybody who
has kissed a lady knows it's true,
that there's no pleasure so complete
as kissing ladies fair and sweet.

541   The mass was over soon and I
with many a pretty one close by
went from the church but then we found
a teeming throng was all around,
the streets were swarming with the crowd.
Before us ladies, long and loud,
a mighty trumpet blast rang out;
the throng was pleased without a doubt.

542   We came back to the inn again
and at the door I parted then
from all that lovely company,
I was as happy as can be.
That God would care for me they prayed
and from their hearts invoked His aid—
it's brought me luck in many a task.
God grants such ladies what they ask.

545   To the Piave rode our band
where, on a pretty meadowland,
I saw awaiting me a knight.
I recognized him at first sight—
Sir Reinprecht von Murecke, a name
that all fair ladies should acclaim
for he made all of them his own
and seldom ever slept alone.

546   The wealthy man was of this ilk.
His shirt was made from finest silk
and it was just as white as snow.
No other armor did he show
but only helmet, spear, and shield;
clad thus he galloped down the field.
His horse was seen enveloped in
rich velvet cloth and baldachin.

547 I had to change my clothes, of course;
he stopped and waited on his horse.
It was no time at all, I guess,
till I had on my battle dress.
I tied my helmet with a band
and took a goodly spear in hand
(of middle size and painted white).
The prospect filled me with delight.

548 His reins were hanging loose and low,
his spear gave off a golden glow,
beneath his arm he let it lie;
I held mine upright on my thigh.
His spear came through my shield and broke
to many pieces with the stroke;
I never lowered mine to thrust.
That's how we both performed the joust.

549 We did as well as any can.
I gave the very wealthy man
a little ring which was of gold;
he earned it well, as I have told,
and tendered me the thanks he owed.
Hermann von Plintenbach next rode
against me, three Italians then,
which made them happy-hearted men.

550 They all rode daringly and well
and since no rider missed or fell
to each was readily allowed
a ring, of which they seemed quite proud.
I broke a spear with every one
and just as soon as this was done
we hurried on so that I might
within Sacile spend the night.

551 No better welcome could one find
for all the balconies were lined
with ladies. I was well received
and didn't feel at all aggrieved.
I went to bed and rested from
the journey. When the day had come
I rose at once, made haste to don
my battle dress and travelled on.

552   Before a very pretty wood
already waited then the good
Meinhart von Gorze and a lot
of knights whose names I've long forgot.
Twelve were wearing helmets then;
as I saw this I told my men,
"Here are some knights who want to joust.
We'll give them what they like, I trust."

553   I changed my horses speedily,
they handed up my shield to me,
I quickly bound my helmet fast,
and took a spear in hand at last.
Meanwhile the knights had ridden near.
The count broke off a shining spear
when it upon my helmet smote—
I shattered mine against his throat.

554   Seven lances broke that day
on me and in as skilled a way
as any noble could desire.
With spirits rising ever higher
I broke eleven, quite a few,
and in a courtly manner too.
Five knights there were who failed to hit
me square and got no ring for it.

555   When I stopped jousting and unbound
my helmet, quickly all around
a lot of other jousts began.
The Count of Gorze struck a man
and knocked his helmet off. I know
I never saw a finer blow.
The fellow almost lost his seat
and fell beneath the horse's feet.

556   A hundred knights were on the field
to show their skilfulness and wield
their lances in the courtly game.
For love of ladies and of fame
some gallant men so bravely fought
that they served ladies as one ought.
This knight was glad, another one
had only grief when all was done.

557   I had to leave, for it was late.
The knights began to separate;
some were so kind and courteous
they rode to St. Odorico with us—
't was there I planned to spend the night.
The next day, when the morning light
drove off the darkness with its power,
we didn't tarry there an hour.

558   I quickly put my armor on
and shortly afterwards was gone.
I sought the field with spears of white
and wished to joust with any knight
who'd come to serve his lady fair.
One knight, of whom I'd heard, was there
who had with him his lady's veil.
He'd want to tourney without fail.

559   Sir Otte von Spengenberg was he,
a noble knight, who rode toward me
with gleaming armor, richly dressed
as fits a lady's suitor best.
His trappings glittered far and wide,
around his helmet there was tied
a veil of an expensive kind,
and thus came he of lofty mind.

560   We both would serve a lady dear;
each had a very heavy spear
and wished to ride a lengthy course.
He hoped to knock me from my horse
and I thought also, "When we meet
I'll see if he can hold his seat.
He will if he would keep his name
untouched by either scorn or shame."

561   Toward me the rider quickly swept—
his spear sank low the horse so leapt.
I turned a little from the man
(to knock him sprawling was my plan)
and swerved back onto him again;
I struck him in the collar then.
I turned and jousted with such skill
Sir Otte almost took a spill.

562   You can believe me that he broke
a sturdy spear against my cloak
and with the lances' crashing sound
a lot of splinters flew around.
His reins and stirrups at the blow
were lost. He seized the saddlebow
at once and with its help could rise.
He would have fallen otherwise.

563   Five others followed, all did well.
They broke their spears and no one fell,
so I gave each of them a ring
and then untied my helmet string
for at Gemona we should stay.
A knight was waiting on the way.
He had a handsome tent pitched where
it overlooked the thoroughfare.

564   Sir Mathie was the noble's name.
He strove for honor and for fame
and many virtues he displayed.
He sent to me a lovely maid
who met our company before
we'd travelled far. A lance she bore
in hand and rode a pretty steed.
Her clothes were very fine indeed.

565   This pure and charming maiden said
(on seeing me) with lips of red,
"Queen Venus, let me welcome you!
Sir Mathie sends me hither to
announce from him that hereabout
you're really welcome. There's no doubt
he's glad to see you. Know that I
tell what he said and not a lie.

566   "My lord has also sent me here
to bring you, lady fair, this spear
and, as his messenger, request
that you would break it on his breast.
This favor he commanded me
to ask with every courtesy.
So take it, lady, if you care
to honor women everywhere."

567   I took the spear which she had brought
and thanked her warmly, as one ought,
for bringing me these words. I bade
a servant say that I'd be glad
to grant the favor she did ask
and willingly perform the task.
The maiden thanked me much for this
and then departed, filled with bliss.

568   I armed myself when she was gone.
I tied my helmet firmly on
and quickly seized a spear and shield.
Then he came riding o'er the field.
'T was thus that I first came to know
this knight who longed for honor so.
His dress was costly at our meeting;
he well deserved a lady's greeting.

570   We soon were not so far apart
and it was time for us to start
a charge or it would be too late.
Both his concern and mine were great
that his should be a pretty joust
and that he'd not fall in the dust.
We spurred together for the stroke
and neither spear remained unbroke.

571   The joust was splendid, I declare.
I knocked his helmet through the air.
The veil he'd fastened to his lance
was hanging from my shield, by chance;
a broad and gaping hole now marred
the shield where it was meant to guard
the shoulder bone on my left side.
It was a joust to suit his pride.

572   He got his helmet back again.
I noticed others riding then
toward me, a half-a-dozen strong.
The spears were neither thick nor long
which each one carried in his hand.
In turn I jousted with the band
and did not miss a single one.
Four had struck me when all was done.

574   That eve while resting at an inn
I saw knights coming to begin
a combat, which was very good.
They rode as well as any could
and tourneyed right in front of me.
No knightly game could ever be
more lively or reveal more skill.
I watched it from my window sill.

576   And when at last the game was o'er
at my command a servant bore
the knights good wine, and quite a lot,
for after labor men have got
a thirst. I treated every soul
in goblet, cup, and silver bowl.
They bowed to me with courtly grace
and went to find their resting place.

577   My steward took four dresses out
to have them washed some place about.
A lady learned to whom he went;
at once the lovely lady sent
the laundress who was there a dress
and bade her by her happiness
to hide it under those of mine.
On it there was a buckle fine.

578   A jeweled band, a belt, a note
were wrapped therein. Though she who wrote
and sent the gifts was virtuous,
without my will she acted thus.
The clothing then was folded so
my steward wasn't apt to know
all that was there. And so he brought
away more dresses than he thought.

579   He took the gifts with my attire,
for which he later earned my ire.
Night passed, the sun came into view.
I went to church but no one knew.
On my return I soon was clad
in battle dress, the best I had.
I never until then had worn
such splendid things as on that morn.

580   My buglers played a melody,
       a pretty tune in a treble key,
       and thus they told all people near
       that I was shortly to appear.
       Then many a proud, high-minded man
       in battle dress at once began
       to leave the houses. They revealed
       themselves with helmet, spear, and shield.

583   Thirty knights or more soon came
       out of the town to start a game.
       In fine array and galloping
       they spurred their horses to the ring.
       The men fought well on either side
       and many noble riders tried
       to break their store of spears in haste.
       The tourney's object was this waste.

584   The knights were jousting all around
       till splinters almost hid the ground
       and several shields lay there as well
       which during fierce encounter fell.
       I charged eleven knights that day
       and broke a lance in each affray
       but two. I finally untied
       my helmet band and rode aside.

585   To seven knights could I accord
       a ring. 'T was thought a great reward
       and those who won the prizes then
       by jousting well were happy men,
       but those whose lances hadn't broke
       seemed angry every time they spoke.
       That they had missed me and thus had
       not won a present made them sad.

586   Gemona soon was left behind
       and many nobles I had wined
       took leave with knightly courtesy.
       The ones who came with us were three:
       Sir Heinrich of Lüenz rode along
       and two Italians, brave and strong,
       whose names I now cannot recall.
       Good men they were, respected all.

587 At Chiusa I passed the night
and just as soon as it was light
I tourneyed with Sir Heinrich, who
was praised by all, as well I knew.
So were his fellows; those who served
me gave them rings, which they deserved.
And so in company like this
six lances broke without a miss.

588 That day my heart could feel no woe.
We travelled to Tarvisio
but there I found no jousting since
Carinthia's most noble prince
had conquered in the selfsame night
with all the country's martial might
a Castle Goldberg. He employed
his men to have the place destroyed.

589 I went next morning with the dawn
before the city. Resting on
a pretty meadow, broad and green,
the vassals and the prince were seen.
They'd halted to have breakfast there;
he liked to eat in the open air.
At least a hundred knights, no less,
were with their ruler, I would guess.

591 The prince and vassals on the ground
then heard my bugles' piercing sound.
They asked, "Who's coming to us, who?"
One said, "The queen is passing through
just as her letter said she would."
Another spoke, "She's welcome! Good!
We'll receive her very well."
Their reception thus befell:

592 The prince and all his company
together warmly welcomed me
in Slavic, "Venus, may our God
receive you!" With a friendly nod
I returned the greeting of the men.
They had my servant ask me then
if I had come to them to joust.
I answered, "Yes, and soon, I trust."

593 Many a good and sturdy man
arose directly and began
to arm himself and soon were dressed
full fifty riders in their best.
All wished to tourney, it was clear;
each quickly got a shield and spear.
I too was now prepared to ride
and filled with confidence and pride.

594 The first to come was richly decked
in all the splendor you'd expect
of one of the prince's favorites.
Sir Hermann, Lord of Osterwitz,
thus was the kindly noble named.
For many virtues rightly famed,
a man of spirit and desire,
no one could value honor higher.

595 We charged as though we wished to slay
each other there. "Give way! Give way!"
I heard the knights around us shout.
It was a most successful bout:
they all could see the lances break
against our heads, and no mistake.
The sparks flew from our helmet so
the others thanked us for the show.

596 I got another weapon from
my squire at once. The next to come
at me was Kol von Finkenstein.
His joust was also very fine.
It certainly was not by chance
that he so deftly broke his lance
against my helmet; he could wield
a spear! I broke mine on his shield.

597 I'll tell you how it went in short
and yet shall give a true report.
On me broke fifteen spears before
the morning ended and no more.
The knights who held them jousted well;
if I the names of all should tell
to whom their ladies' thanks were due
my tale would be too long for you.

598   Eighteen lances for my part
I broke and with a happy heart
at last untied my helmet strings
and quickly gave out fifteen rings
to those who'd jousted well that day.
This done, I started on the way
to Villach and without a care.
The folks were glad to see me there.

600   The rooms at Villach which we had
were very nice, and I was glad.
At dawn I left the inn to pass
a morning hour hearing mass;
in woman's clothing I was dressed
and wore, of course, my very best.
I tripped to church so merrily
that many had to laugh at me.

601   When I returned from there I ate
my breakfast. Since it wasn't late
I looked to see what I should wear
the next few days. Without a care,
my heart was light, my spirit gay.
I checked on all the skirts that lay
in front of me, and all was fine
till I found one that wasn't mine.

602   When I beheld it on the bed
I called my steward in and said,
"Now tell me who has dared to give
me this, if you would like to live."
He spoke, "My lady, I don't know.
I think it most peculiar though.
Who gave the skirt and who could bring
it so you'd not observe a thing?"

603   Without delay I then unbound
the skirt and this is what I found:
a buckle, belt, and jeweled band;
I've ne'er had finer in my hand.
There was a German letter too
which made my wrath break forth anew.
I told the steward then, "You should
believe, for you this means no good."

604 "My dearest lady," he replied,
"do let your anger now subside.
I do not know (and hope to die
if this is false) who brought them by."
I took the letter, opened it,
and had him read what there was writ.
He read the message, which explained
the presents. Hear what it contained:

"Noble Venus, I extend
a greeting and would like to lend
to you my service faithfully.
All ladies everywhere should be
grateful that you in friendliness
have put on you a woman's dress
and thereby honored womankind.
May all our praises be assigned
to you. I hope that you will prize
these gifts of mine and not despise
what I have sent for love of you.
I must remain unknown, it's true,
because discretion counsels it.
If you are honored, I admit
that I am happy, very much,
my thought regarding you is such.
God guard your honor, stand beside you,
and on your knightly journeys guide you,
may nothing needful be denied you."

605 Just as I heard the letter read
a messenger appeared and said
to me, "Most noble queen, I'd say
you ought to arm without delay.
And I must tell you anyhow,
the knights are all quite ready now
and riding to the field nearby.
Their messenger to you am I."

606   I spoke, "I'm glad that they are here."
I put my armor on with cheer
and soon was all prepared to go
in battle dress as white as snow.
I rode at once into the field
and found with armor, lance, and shield
some forty knights awaiting me.
That they would joust was plain to see.

610   "Crash!" and "Crash!" It filled the air
upon the common everywhere.
The riders tourneyed fast and hard;
the ground was covered with many a shard.
I broke a spear at every run,
fifteen in all; when this was done
I went back to the inn again
and sent twelve rings out to the men

611   who'd earned a prize from me that day.
I put my armor all away
and donned a woman's dress and hat
and on the balcony I sat.
But when they saw me—listen well
and you shall know what then befell—
a knightly game of war began,
including every single man.

613   The evening now began to fade.
From early morning they had stayed
in armor which was hard and tight
and many of them longed for night
who suffered much from weariness.
Yet others there felt no distress
and wished to serve their ladies more,
but darkness fell; the game was o'er.

614   The next day was the third, and I
soon was ready to say goodbye
and with my train to journey on.
I was quite anxious to be gone
and in a happy frame of mind
when we left Villach far behind.
Twenty good nobles with me rode
to Feldkirchen, my next abode.

615   A lot of people were aware
of when I'd promised to be there.
They rode in from the countryside
to see me, came from far and wide
with shining armor and richly dressed.
I'll name you several of the best.
To joust with me came Sir Gottfried
von Havenerburg, a knight indeed.

616   His brother, Sir Arnold, also came.
It wasn't long till both could claim
a ring; 't was earned with a valiant thrust.
Sir Kol von Treven was there to joust
and Bernhart and Ulrich von Treven too.
Von Himmelberg, a noble who
(the bold Sir Zacheus was he)
was known for song and poetry,

617   had come there wearing on his back,
over his armor, cloth of black.
He wore a monk's cape; it was big
and on his helmet was a wig
in which a tonsure had been shorn.
With many oaths the knight had sworn
he'd knock Queen Venus from her horse,
and that was his intent, of course.

618   I faced eleven knights, and they
had skill and courage to display.
I broke a spear on each of ten,
and every one of these good men
broke off his lance on me. That's right.
I then beheld the monkish knight;
he rode toward me inside the ring
but that was quite a useless thing.

619   When I beheld him coming so
I took my helmet off to go
and sent a messenger to tell
him, since he liked such cloth so well
and seemed a monk and not a knight,
the queen did not believe it right
to joust with him. Chivalric sport
was not for people of his sort.

74

620   I rode back to the hostelry
where food and ease awaited me.
I went to bed when day was done,
and in the morning as the sun
shone brightly down I journeyed thence.
The monk had caused me some offense
and I took care my anger showed.
Ere long into St. Veith we rode.

621   While we were still some distance out
my coming was proclaimed about,
and some decided not to wait
but welcome me before the gate.
Their joyful greeting I commend;
they met me as one meets a friend,
their words were courteous and good.
I bowed as warmly as I could.

622   We rode to town with great delight.
I asked a servant bid who might
desire to joust with me begone
and come back with his armor on.
At this the nobles all were glad,
and twenty-five of them soon had
armor and spear, and would employ
them both to seek renown and joy.

625   At once upon the field I came
and found the ones who longed for fame
awaiting me with shield and spear
so they might do some jousting here.
Without delay I took a lance
and saw a worthy knight advance,
Sir Reinher von Eichelsberg was he,
a man of honor and honesty.

626   We both performed a pretty joust,
and neither tumbled in the dust.
We proved ourselves both sharp of eye—
the splinters of our spears flew high.
As soon as this fine joust was through
Sir Konrad von Lebnach rode into
the circle; brave and in the prime
of life, he won much praise in time.

627   Then came Sir Kone von Friedberg, in might
and skill with arms a noble knight
but not with property or gold
(that's what those who knew him told).
Sir Jacob von Berg who spent his days
in seeking for renown and praise
tourneyed with me and won a prize.
Sir Konrad von Teinach did likewise.

630   The monk appeared again at last
inside the circle. He held fast
a heavy weapon in his hand;
to joust with me he took his stand.
When I beheld the monkish cloak
and recognized him, thus I spoke,
"I shall not meet you, I declare
and truly, here or anywhere."

631   I took my helmet off and went
to the inn, where I could rest content
from all my labors. There I lay
until the breaking of the day.
We packed to leave; but, nonetheless,
I first put on my battle dress
and asked a squire to find out how
the knights would like to tourney now.

632   When my intentions were revealed
they came with helmet, lance, and shield.
Six were waiting and no more
with spear in hand before the door,
ready for jousting to begin.
When I beheld them from the inn,
each one as eager as a squire,
I thought, "You'll get what you desire."

633   At once I took a spear in hand
to joust the first one of the band;
it was Sir Ortold von Osterwitz.
His lance and mine were broke to bits
and splinters scattered high and low
we raced against each other so.
The joust was good, both lances smote
and shattered squarely on the throat.

634   Sir Wichard von Karlsberg took his place
but rode at much too slow a pace
and didn't break his spear on me.
The next one galloped valiantly,
Sir Engelram von Strassburg; I
rode just as fast and that is why
his joust soon brought him his reward.
Then came Sir Engelbrecht, a Lord

635   of Strassburg and a worthy knight
to whom high praises brought delight;
his manners were refined indeed.
The next to joust was Sir Siegfried,
the Saxon, as the lord was named,
who in Carinthia was famed
and truly never did amiss;
he won a lot of friends for this.

636   Once more the knight in monkish guise
appeared. He hoped to win the prize
from me of all the goods I had.
My messenger did as I bade
and quickly went to him to say
that while he wore a monk's array
I would not meet him, for it must
offend my honor should we joust.

637   The monk addressed the messenger,
"Then I shall follow after her
to every place she may appear,
none has the right to interfere.
She's going to prove to me her skill;
I am determined that she will,
and only death can hinder it.
No pain could change my mind a bit.

638   The knights were very courteous
but came to me and all spoke thus,
"Lady, we pray that you'll allow
that we politely beg you now
to grant the wish of this monk here
and, jousting with him, break a spear;
for, no matter how he's dressed,
he seeks for honor as do the rest."

639   I said, "Since you have asked me to
    I'll grant him this, but just for you.
    I got a spear and rode my horse
    where it could run a lengthy course.
    You can believe me when I tell
    you that I did not like him well
    and was resolved that I'd take care
    to strike him on the head, and square.

640   I'll tell you quickly what transpired.
    He broke his lance as he desired,
    but I delivered such a blow
    he landed in the dirt below
    and lay unconscious from the fall,
    which didn't worry me at all.
    Many were glad of it; thereafter
    his fall provoked a lot of laughter.

641   I'd struck his helmet as I'd planned
    with all the strength at my command.
    To him and to the others I
    gave fourteen rings and said goodbye.
    I left the city and began
    my journey as a happy man.
    We came to Friesach—in the gown
    of Venus I rode into town.

645   The knights were riding with a will
    and wielding spears with knightly skill,
    a lot of shields were broke that day.
    The noble riders' courtly play
    continued till 't was almost night
    and all their steeds with foam were white.
    When day and evening both were past
    the knights gave up their sport at last.

646   But soon enough the night was gone
    and with the coming of the dawn
    once more they dressed them for a game
    in armor, and I did the same.
    Onto the field we hastened then;
    I was the happiest of men
    since I could serve my lady fair
    that day before the nobles there.

647   On the field before the gate
I saw Sir Konrad von Nidecke wait,
adorned as worthy knights should be.
He made a gallant charge at me,
his course was long and did not waver,
he sought to earn a lady's favor
and spurred his charger to great speed.
Mine too was not so slow indeed.

648   I'll tell you how the tourney went.
He broke his spear just as he meant
and on my throat I felt it land.
I wounded him in his right hand,
which really caused me great distress
because of his true nobleness.
He was a valiant knight, it's true,
fearless and manly through and through.

649   Sir Otto and Sir Dietrich, Lords
of Buches, earned them no rewards
and there were angry murmurings
because they both had lost their rings.
Their hearts were·strongly set on gain;
they wished for riches more, 't was plain,
than lover's pay of any kinds.
Broad fields and meadows filled their minds.

650   On seven knights I broke a spear
and promptly journeyed forth from here.
Five golden rings to them were sent.
who'd jousted well before I went
along toward Scheifling with my band
in Styria, a lovely land.
Nineteen nobles travelled down
with us. Five waited in the town.

652   In Scheifling then I passed the night.
When it was banished by the light
of day I rose and soon was dressed
in armor, as were all the rest
who'd come to share our knightly sport.
On all of them the richest sort
of robes and armor were revealed.
At once we hastened to the field.

653   Of such as these I'm glad to tell.
The first had clothed him very well
as any courtly noble must
who knows good manners and can joust.
Sir Ilsung von Scheifling was his name;
his heart has never ceased to claim
those things which make one good and wise.
He sought to win a worthy prize.

654   Five hundred bells and maybe more
the lofty-minded noble wore.
With little bounds his charger sprang
and as he moved the metal rang
until one couldn't hear a word.
The gleaming gold and silver sherd
was on a red and green brocade
and all was very nicely made.

655   My countryman was decked so fine
that not a knight along the Rhine
was ever better dressed, and few
as well; what I have said is true.
The spear he carried in his hand
was decorated with a band
to which were fastened bells, but all
of these were really very small.

656   So often and so well he strove
that one might call him Waste-The-Grove.
He spurred his horse into a race
and then a pretty joust took place.
My shield went flying with his stroke,
for all the thongs which held it broke.
Like thunder did the joust resound;
the shield was lying on the ground.

657   My spear was snapped in two on him
just as a dry and heavy limb
bent down and broken from a tree.
I do not think there'll ever be
from jousting such a mighty crack
as sounded forth from our attack.
The bells flew all around like dust,
the shields were shattered by the joust.

658   As soon as this fine course was run
       four others followed, one by one,
       and then I gave away five rings.
       I heard them say, "Queen Venus brings
       us on her journey sport and cheer.
       God has preserved her well till here;
       may He protect her from all foes
       in tenderness where'er she goes."

659   Toward Judenburg at once I went
       with spirits high and pleasure bent,
       but still I wished that things were so
       that my dear lady fair might know
       how she had occupied my mind.
       For I thought thus, "She is so kind,
       if she discovered how I felt
       toward her alone her heart would melt."

660   In Judenburg they greeted me
       with eagerness; immediately
       I thanked them with a friendly air.
       They gave a hearty welcome there.
       I had a quiet place to stay
       that night and with the break of day
       I donned my armor, bright and strong.
       I didn't wish to tarry long.

661   Bedecked I rode onto the field
       where nine good knights also revealed
       their costly trappings, arms, and dress.
       They were the soul of courtliness.
       I broke nine spears on them, and this
       was done without a single miss.
       Three knights missed me, their aim was bad,
       which didn't make them very glad.

662   I gave the six the rings I owed,
       and then without delaying rode
       toward Knittelfeld, with joy to tour
       on down the valley of the Mur.
       The morrow came and then I broke
       two spears soon after I awoke
       and gave two golden rings away.
       My thoughts dwelt on a lover's pay.

663   To Leoben I travelled then
and found there twenty noblemen
awaiting me with spirits high.
When we rode in the city I
was well received by every knight
for all were friendly and polite.
The courtesies which there I viewed
deserved in truth my gratitude.

664   Dismounting at the inn at last,
I rested till the night was past.
That morning when the sun arose,
from every alley, I suppose,
I heard the flute's delightful sound
and saw the knights from all around
gayly to a meadow streaming
with rich apparel brightly gleaming.

666   I rode upon the meadow land
and took a shining spear in hand.
Sir Dietmar von Steier was to face
me first; he galloped to his place.
We came together at great speed;
you should have seen our spears indeed—
we both had struck so hard and well
in tiny bits to earth they fell.

667   Then came Sir Siegfried von Torsiol;
he had a brave and manly soul,
and all his limbs were tough and strong.
He never did one any wrong
and acted as a noble should.
His joust with me, of course, was good.
Both of our lances broke thereby;
all there could see the splinters fly.

668   I'll tell you all, but make it short;
while we pursued this knightly sport
were thirteen lances broke on me.
Since I'm to tell it truthfully,
I missed three times in tourneying.
At once I gave each knight a ring
who'd jousted well and so had won
a prize from me. When this was done

669   we journeyed on from Leoben's walls
to where the Mürz's water falls
into the Mur with rush and roar.
They catch the fish there by the score.
Now up the stream I rode until
a castle towers on a hill—
Kapfenberg—high and alone.
In all of Styria it's known.

670   The master of it was a lord
whose will was constantly set toward
the things a noble ought to do
to win acclaim; all these he knew.
He was generous, his name
was guarded carefully from shame;
he was dauntless and well-bred.
I haven't lied in what I've said.

671   He followed honor faithfully.
Sir Wülfing von Stubenberg was he
and rich in people and in lands;
he had those things which wealth commands.
Sir Wülfing, when he came to know
of my arrival down below,
declared, "As soon as I have seen
her I shall greet the noble queen."

678   When he was ready to receive
me thirty knights (so I believe)
came with him. Down the hill they rode,
well-clad and in the courtly mode.
Before I travelled to this meeting
I'd never had a warmer greeting
than I was given by this knight
at Kapfenberg. While it was light,

679   unarmed, but dressed in bright array
I sought the place where I would stay
and rest in comfort till the dawn.
When day had come and night was gone
I put my armor on again.
My longing, loving heart was then
filled with gladness and content,
which made itself quite evident.

680   When I was clothed and at the last
had tied my helmet on me fast
I rode to the field with festive air.
The Knight of Stubenberg was there
and was in all so richly dressed
that I was very much impressed.
His splendid armor gleamed on him
and nearly made the sun look dim.

681   The proud and gallant noble rode
toward me, and all his trappings glowed
as if he came from heaven's door.
His skill had many times before
won highest praises, I'd been told.
His course was very swift and bold;
his horse so close to mine was guided
that he and I almost collided.

682   The points of both our spears were thrust
right through our bucklers with the joust
so that a noisy crash rang out
and bits of lances flew about
as well as parts of each man's shield.
His sleeve as well as mine concealed
a bruise; some rings of armor fell.
The joust was ridden hard and well.

684   A lot of spears were shattered then;
I broke a dozen on the men.
It went as I had wished it to
and I'd not missed when we were through.
The worthy nobles rode at me
twelve times and each so skilfully
that no one failed to break his spear.
Twelve golden rings I gave out here.

703   I had a place to spend the night.
As soon as all was clear and light
and sunbeams shone on everything
I climbed across the Semmering
to Gloggnitz on the other side.
I found six nobles there astride
their mounts who wished to try their skill
and I was quick to do their will.

704 They rode toward me with armor on;
I had not waited long to don
a rich and splendid battle dress.
Von Ringenberg with full success
broke off a spear on me. The one
I jousted with when this was done
I knocked down backwards off his horse,
which made him feel ashamed, of course.

706 The spears I broke then numbered four.
On the field had come no more
with armor on and lance in hand
and so I stopped. At my command
the servants gave six rings away.
I sought the inn where I should stay
and found a pretty hostel there;
I got some other things to wear.

707 I changed my clothing under guard,
and then the hostel door was barred.
I took with me a servant who
would not say anything, I knew.
We stole away without a sound
and rode with joy to where I found
my dearest wife whom I adore;
I could not ever love her more.

708 She greeted me just as a good
and loving woman always should
receive a husband she holds dear.
That I had come to see her here
had made her really very pleased.
My visit stilled her grief and eased
her loneliness. We shared our bliss,
my sweet and I, with many a kiss.

709 She was so glad to see her knight,
and I had comfort and delight
till finally the third day came;
to give me joy was her sole aim.
When dawn appeared it was the third.
I dressed, an early mass was heard,
I prayed God keep me from transgressing,
and then received a friendly blessing.

710   Right after that I took my leave,
lovingly, you may believe,
and rode with joyful heart to where
I'd left my servants unaware.
I entered Gloggnitz hastily
and found them waiting there for me,
prepared to journey on again.
At once we left the city then.

711   We rode to Neunkirchen gaily decked
and were received as I'd expect
of those whose manners are refined.
Each knight was courteous and kind
who waited there with spear and shield.
When I came riding on the field
I found them all prepared, adorned
with trappings no one would have scorned.

712   Nine waited there, not more nor less,
to joust with me, in battle dress.
I saw them and it wasn't long
till I'd donned armor, bright and strong.
The first to come I'd heard much of;
his great desire was ladies' love.
It was Sir Ortold von Graz, a name
already widely known to fame.

713   All that he wore was of the best.
The good man cut me in the chest
so strong and skilful was his joust;
through shield and armor went the thrust.
When I beheld the wound indeed
and saw that it began to bleed
I hid it quickly with my coat
before the other knights took note.

715   I broke nine lances there in haste
and found my inn. I dared not waste
much time before I got in bed.
I sent nine rings of golden red
to each of them who with his spear
had earned from me a present here.
My injuries were deftly bound
by a doctor whom my servants found.

716   His presence there was soon found out;
      ere long the tale was spread about
      that Venus had been wounded sore
      and so that she could joust no more.
      The knights were sad to lose their sport,
      but when I heard the false report
      I said, "Tomorrow I shall stay
      a while ere going on my way.

717   "I'd like to let the people see
      the truth in what is said of me
      and know that I am well and strong.
      Although the tale is not all wrong
      this little wound will quickly heal
      and I can easily conceal
      it so that none will be aware
      that I've been injured by a hair."

718   There it was I spent the night,
      but when the second day was bright
      and when the sun shone in the skies
      I did what I considered wise
      and donned my woman's finery
      to look as pretty as could be
      in lady's dress as white as snow.
      I went to church so all would know.

719   Whoever saw me gaily walk
      to church that morning thus would talk,
      "It must be false what people tell;
      this queen is light of heart and well,
      her thoughts are gay, her step is strong."
      I left the church with such a throng
      around me when the mass was o'er
      that truly they knocked down the door.

720   To serve my love and lady then
      I would have liked to joust again
      but found that all the knights were gone,
      so joyfully we travelled on
      till Wiener Neustadt was in view.
      I'd often told my retinue,
      they need no gaiety suppress:
      "Good manners go with happiness."

727 　And thus I entered with my train
　　　the town. I called my chamberlain
　　　and bade him have someone prepare
　　　a water bath for me somewhere
　　　outside of town and tell no one.
　　　I came as soon as this was done,
　　　got in the bath my man had hired
　　　and soon forgot that I was tired.

729 　When I climbed in and sat me down
　　　my steward started back to town
　　　to go into the inn and find
　　　some clothing he had left behind.
　　　In truth you must believe me that
　　　without a servant there I sat
　　　which makes me think at any rate
　　　that what's to come will never wait.

730 　And I believe without a doubt
　　　that what's to be will come about.
　　　I learned then some of what this meant
　　　and now I'll tell you how it went.
　　　As I was sitting there alone
　　　a page came up I'd never known—
　　　clever, courtly, and well-clad.
　　　I'll tell you what the fellow had.

731 　This smart young man, without a sign
　　　or word, put down a carpet fine;
　　　before my bath the carpet lay.
　　　He placed thereon a woman's array:
　　　a skirt, a heavy veil were there
　　　(there were no better anywhere),
　　　a belt as nice as I have seen,
　　　a buckle which would suit a queen,

732 　a head-band, bright and glittering,
　　　a ruby set into a ring,
　　　red as a lovely lady's lips
　　　which wound a heart the while it skips.
　　　He placed a letter on the stone,
　　　with pretty words it should make known
　　　the one who sent these gifts to me,
　　　so he informed me carefully.

733   When I beheld them by my bath
my mouth spoke up with honest wrath,
"Say, to whom were these things brought?
I'll tell you plainly. I've no thought,
believe me, either clothes or gem,
of taking even one of them.
So take them out, whate'er you do,
for I am really vexed with you."

734   The page departed unconcerned
but with two others soon returned
who bore rose petals, gleaming red,
and these, without a word being said,
were scattered on me by the youth
until they were so thick, in truth,
that bath and I were covered o'er.
He would not utter one word more.

735   Despite my pleading and my rage
I got more petals from the page
so that the floor around was soon
quite lovely with the petals strewn.
Thereon he bowed and, though he heard
a lot from me, he said no word
but only turned and went away.
I'd never seen him till that day.

736   He left me angry and harassed.
My chamberlain returned at last
and brought a robe and towels to dry
me with. He saw the gifts nearby
and spoke, "My great and noble queen,
what's this? And what do these things mean?
But you're completely covered o'er
and roses color all the floor!"

737   I told him, "You're to blame. 'T was wrong
to leave me all alone so long
and it's a fault I must condemn.
Some pages brought these things with them:
the roses, jewels, and the dress.
The youth who led them, I confess,
I do not know, neither his name
nor the place from which he came.

738   "This makes me very angry still
for every bit against my will
he laid these things down by my side.
Such deeds as this I can't abide
and never saw before, I vow.
But just give me my bathrobe now;
there'll be no bath for me, and I
shall leave these presents where they lie."

739   Then spoke my chamberlain to me,
"Good lady, no, that must not be.
It truly would be wrong, I fear,
were you to leave these presents here.
Those working in the place would claim
them and would soon find out the name
of her whose love has sent them. No,
't would not be right to leave them so.

740   "Perhaps she has a lot of friends,
then you might never make amends
if you should cause her any pain
by letting what she sent remain
in here. So let me keep this prize,
in truth I think that this is wise.
And hear, it's also good for you
to be most careful what you do,

741   "that you protect yourself and her
for it may be a messenger
will come and tell you who has sent
the gifts which you so much resent
and you can then return them still.
Let me advise you if you will.
She's fond of you, that one can tell,
for this one ought to treat her well."

742   "I'll let you take the things away
but take them only that I may,
just as soon as it is known
who sends me clothes and precious stone,
return the presents I receive;
and this you may as well believe.
I can not keep a thing they've brought
or else my constancy were naught.

743   "I've always heard that no one can
give to a woman or a man
a present quite against their will.
My mind would certainly be ill
should I accept what one bestows
who's not the lady that I chose
to be the one for whom I live.
I want what she alone can give."

744   I left the bath house then and rode
in secret to the town and strode
into the inn where I should stay.
I didn't go outside that day
and wore a solemn face long after
for angry spirits bear no laughter.
This truth I easily could guess
in seeking that day's happiness.

746   I thought, "I'll get someone to read
the letter. It may be indeed
the lady's name is written there."
'T was read to me and, I declare,
that note did credit to the sender.
It's greeting, though it was quite tender,
did not affect me much when read,
but listen to what the letter said:

"Lady, could I shape the phrases
to greet you well with sweetest praises,
I'd do it, on my word, serene
Venus, fair and noble queen.
Because of your nobility
true service you shall have from me.
For well do you indeed deserve
that noble women all should serve
you with praise unceasing,
your honor thus increasing.
To honor you have turned each thought
and so to you my gifts were brought
that both of us may gain
more honor. Lady, deign
to keep the presents I impart,
remembering your kindly heart.

They're sent to you for honor alone
and I desire to be unknown
because I must be circumspect;
may you, dear lady, not object.
If my wishes might come true
and should my eyes soon gaze on you
then I myself will let you know
why I have sent these presents so
to you, my dearest lady fair.
I now commend you to the care
of Him who came our ways to straighten
and whose power conquered Satan,
our adversary grim.
May He take you to Him
and give you many honors here;
this is the hope sincere
of my heart and mind.
In my loyal heart I find
a wish that you will reap the best
on this honor-bringing quest."

748   What more is there for me to say?
I felt sorrow and dismay,
with anger I was quite distressed
and got that night so little rest
that I was rather ill and worn.
But with the coming of the morn
I heard an early mass and then
festively set out again.

749   Toward Austria and down the plain
I led a very courtly train.
When we approached the Piesting Stream
of shining shields I caught a gleam.
Soon after there appeared in sight
well-trimmed helmets and spears of white.
The nobles riding toward this meeting
received me with a friendly greeting.

751   The names of some of those I'll tell
who welcomed me that day so well.
There were some thirty men of horse,
and one was called Sir Wolfger von Gors.
So virtuous in deed and word
was he that I have never heard
a thing of him that one could blame.
He strove for honor and for fame.

752   The worthy man addressed me there,
"My noble queen and lady fair,
I come to bring you a request
and hope to find my suit is blessed.
I ask, dear queen, that you let me
become one of your company
and through your grace would I obtain
the office of a chamberlain."

753   When I had heard this gallant man
Sir Gottfried von Dozenbach began
(a noble fit for any task),
"Now listen to the boon I ask.
I come here at my lord's command
to bid you welcome to this land
with God, and bring a greeting from
my lord, who's glad that you have come.

754   "Von Regensburg sends it by me.
The bishop's governor is he
and one who values honor too.
Whatever he can do for you
you may be sure he'll not be loath
to do; on this I'll take an oath.
He'll serve you faithfully and for
the ladies' favor, nothing more.

755   "He bids me say that he aspires
to serve you and that he desires,
most noble queen, that you allow
him to be your marshal now.
He's rich in property and thought,
and he will serve you as he ought.
Your worth is such he would persuade
you, lady, to accept his aid."

756   I had a servant answer then
that I'd be glad to have both men:
"But he who seeks an office here
will need to earn it with a spear
and have such skill and temperament
that he will never need lament
because he didn't joust aright.
My office is for such a knight."

758   Sir Wolfger von Gors spoke right away,
"Lady, what more is there to say?
Your court is stately, one can win
great honor for himself therein.
Should I become your chamberlain,
I'll hold the post without a stain
and shall receive it through my skill
at jousting anytime you will."

759   ". . . . [two lines missing] . . . .
   . . . .
There at Traiskirchen we can joust.
In virtue you have put your trust
and are a noble of the sort
I like to have about my court.
You serve the ladies well, and my
respect for you is very high."

760   The good man thanked me then and bowed
with gratitude, for he was proud,
and rode off quickly. He was bound
for Traiskirchen; it was there he found
his armor and his battle steed.
Soon he was well attired indeed
and like an angel to behold.
He wasn't one to save his gold.

761   When he rode away from me,
von Dozenbach spoke courteously,
"My gracious queen, by all adored,
what message shall I bring my lord
from you? I pray that you will show
your kindness and will let me know,
for here I've nothing more to do.
My lord will gladly joust with you."

762 "Tell the governor from me,
would he serve ladies faithfully,
then he may join my retinue.
But if he'd be my marshal too
then he must joust and break his lance;
his honor he may thus advance.
I'll gladly place him in this post
if honor's what he wants the most."

763 The courtly noble didn't wait
but rode to Vienna to relate
to Regensburg without delay
the message given him to say.
His lord was pleased and spent the night
to see that everything was bright
which he and all his riders wore.
They were adorned as ne'er before.

764 But meanwhile I had ridden down
to Traiskirchen. Just before the town
I found awaiting me someone
who never in his life had done
unknightly deeds. It was, of course,
the good Sir Wolfger, Knight of Gors.
His armor gleamed from sunny skies
and threw their radiance in my eyes.

766 I saw him and made haste to don
my armor, tied my helmet on,
and soon was splendidly decked out.
"Give way, my lord!" I heard the shout
and cries of pleasure filled the air
from all the nobles gathered there.
We charged at once with leveled spear;
as soon as I had galloped near

767 to him I spurred to greater speed;
he also quickly urged his steed.
We rode so closely in the joust
and were so skillful in our thrust
that both his shield and mine were shattered
to pieces which were widely scattered.
Against the helmet each man broke
his lance in splinters with the stroke.

768   And so it was my chamberlain
received the post he wished to gain.
Some other knights opposed me then
in courtly manner; there were ten,
and seven of them soon were hailed
by those around, the others failed
to break a spear; their joy was small.
I broke eleven spears in all.

769   I had my servants quickly bring
to each of seven knights a ring;
Sir Wolfger also got his prize.
He was a courtly man and wise
who liked good men and, I've heard tell,
could also please the ladies well,
and with the world it was the same.
He was a man whom none could blame.

770   Such was this chamberlain of mine.
His servants all looked very fine
for they as well were richly clad,
and very courtly dress they had.
On foot the noble came to me
and took my armor so that he
could have a servant clean it right;
he ordered him to get it white.

771   On foot he led my horse around
to where my hostel was. I found
the ease I wanted and a bed.
The courtly nobleman then said,
"My lady, you must have repose."
Whereon he ordered them to close
the hostelry, and this was done.
I wakened with the morning sun.

795   I wore the finest things I could
as I was feeling very good.
I took with me a heavy spear,
and soon a knight came riding near,
von Horschendorf, a sturdy man.
He challenged me and then began
his charge. He wanted to obtain
a ring and jousted only for gain.

796   I'll tell you briefly, it was so:
I broke ten lances in a row
on him, and all he did was miss;
he got quite vexed because of this,
and when we made the final course
he missed once more but struck my horse
right in the head. The wound was bad,
which made the good man very sad.

798   I laid my armor all away
and dressed in feminine array;
I had some lovely clothes to don.
Then to Vienna I rode on
and eighty nobles, good and strong,
in happy spirits went along
with costly gear and richly dressed.
I heard then many a courtly jest.

818   When it was known that I was there
the ladies started to prepare
themselves and many a costly gown
was put on ladies of the town.
They dressed themselves in rivalry
and each was jealous as could be;
who came in more elaborate state
would win another's lasting hate.

819   So fashioned is a woman's mind:
though she be young or old, I find,
she likes to have a lot of dresses.
It is enough if she possesses
the things, they are not just to wear
but rather so she can declare,
"I could, you know, be better dressed
than many who always wear their best."

821   Vienna ladies looked right well
when I rode in, I'm glad to tell.
The streets were filled, as I rode by,
with women, and I won't deny
I thought it really quite a treat.
I saw there many a lady sweet,
and all so warmly welcomed me
that I was happy as can be.

822 We rode along, and when we neared
    my lodging place a knight appeared
    who strove for honor and for fame
    and I shall tell you now his name:
    Sir Hadmar von Kühnringe. With a band
    of errant knights from all the land
    he welcomed me before the inn.
    "Crash!" and "Crash!" They made a din.

823 The welcome soon was going strong;
    before the inn a surging throng
    of knights contested on a field.
    The mighty crash of shield on shield
    was heard from all about, it's true.
    Sir Hadmar and his noisy crew
    received me with their knightly sport.
    I rode into the hostel's court.

824 There was a balcony that faced
    them. Here in woman's dress I placed
    myself. To see me was enough
    to make the sport get pretty rough.
    In groups the riders raced around,
    the field became a battle ground,
    and some collided rather hard.
    The young knights sought to win regard.

825 When I saw horses in the dirt
    and knew that someone would get hurt
    I bade my marshal through a squire
    to ask the riders to retire.
    When he told them of my request
    at once they let the jousting rest.
    They stopped because they wished to please
    and rode then to their hostelries.

826 Soon after came the end of day,
    and all the knights had gone away.
    I wished my courtly page and sent
    for him. When he had come we went
    aside from all the other folk
    and for an hour or two we spoke.
    I said, "My messenger so dear,
    I bid you hearty welcome here.

827   "Now you must tell me, courtly youth,
and not attempt to hide the truth.
How does my lovely lady feel?
I wish to know (do not conceal
a thing) if she is gay or sad
for, if her mood is always glad,
I know my plans will never miss.
She's all my joy, I'm sure of this."

829   In answer quickly spoke the boy,
"She's feeling well and full of joy.
I heard the lady once maintain,
whatever happiness you gain
will make her really glad at heart.
The lady had this to impart,
"Whatever honors him will be
in every way a joy to me."

838   "Dear messenger, I ask a boon
which you must grant me very soon
if it can possibly be done.
Go see again my lovely one
and ask her by the worthiness
which God permits her to possess
to send a gift and her consent
to wear it in a tournament."

840   "Lord and friend, I'll hurry there.
May God help me in this affair!
I'll do the best I can for you.
If the lady fair is willing to
bestow the present you desire,
if I am able to acquire
the gift from her, and if she's kind,
I'll be right back again, you'll find."

841   "Then go! May God not let you slip.
Both there and while you're on the trip
may blessings and good fortune lead;
I pray this from my heart indeed.
If she will send me, as her knight,
a gift 't will be a great delight.
May God go with you now to her,
my friend and faithful messenger."

842   The page departed as he said
he would. I went to find my bed
and there remained until the day
had come to drive the night away.
I heard an early mass, committing
myself to God then, as was fitting.
Without Him honor will not last
until a half a day is past.

843   When I received a blessing there
I left the chapel to prepare
myself and see that all was good
which I put on, as jousters should
who want to guard their bodies well
and are determined to excel.
I hid the armor to the throat
then with a white and folded coat.

848   I left the hostel on my horse
and saw my chamberlain von Gors
with seven squires, all well arrayed.
No clothes could have been better made
than those of his and of his men.
He took my horse's bridle then
and, walking, led it festively.
Many a noble rode with me.

849   About me was a surging throng.
The balconies there all along
were filled with ladies, side by side;
their glances made me satisfied.
I saw then many a lovely form
which made my heart feel gay and warm.
To look at ladies is a pleasure,
their greetings every knight must treasure.

850   We travelled through the city thus.
A hundred nobles came with us,
with splendid gear and clothes they rode,
each knight a handsome steed betrode,
and every piece of metal gleamed.
With happy hearts the riders streamed
along, and singing as they went.
For all it was a gay event.

852   And so I rode upon the field.
        There waited, all prepared to wield
        a lance, the bishop's governor.
        He needed now to wait no more
        and, as I moved toward him, the knight
        tied on his helmet, trimmed and bright;
        his squire then handed him his spear.
        He wished to serve his lady here.

856   Von Gors, my chamberlain, had seen
        and spoke, "My lady, noble queen,
        here comes the governor toward you.
        Now take a spear; whate'er you do,
        sit firmly or you'll come to ill,
        for he has bravery and skill
        and is a very sturdy man.
        He'll surely do the best he can.

857   With care I followed his command;
        he put a spear into my hand.
        The governor began to dash
        at me, another was so rash
        that he raced out in front of him
        (at this the governor was grim).
        Sir Gundacker was the other's name,
        von Stier, and not unknown to fame.

858   This knight rode at me very fast.
        The governor, though he'd been passed,
        continued on, and I could see
        both riders rushing down on me.
        Now was the time to spur my horse
        to charge with all his speed and force.
        I missed the first, as I designed,
        and broke my spear on him behind.

859   Where the helmet meets the shield
        and the collar is revealed,
        right on the throat the man was hit
        so violently the collar split.
        The noble almost lost his seat
        and fell down at the horse's feet.
        We both, of course, regretted this
        and wished my joust had been a miss.

860
That's how I rode my tourney then.
And was I missed by both the men?
No. The knights had jousted well
and each one broke his spear, they fell
in pieces, so it wasn't bad.
The Knight of Stier was very glad
to find that he had earned a ring
from Venus with his tourneying.

861
Soon on the field was such a press
that I was angry, I confess.
They crowded here, they crowded there
and crowded so that I nowhere
could find myself an open space.
'T was hard to joust in such a place.
The course I ran could not be long,
for this there was too great a throng.

862
All wished to break a lance on me
before they left and often three
would charge together, for so great
was their desire they couldn't wait.
You can believe, when I saw that,
I sat as firm as e'er I sat
and prayed that God increase my skill
and save me from a shameful spill.

863
I often had to dodge and dash
in order to avoid a crash;
it took some pretty skilful riding
to keep from frequently colliding.
The field was full of knightly folk.
A lot of lances there were broke
for ladies valiantly that day
and rings of mail were torn away.

902
Soon after to the inn we went
where five-and-thirty rings were sent,
a ring for every gallant knight
who'd earned one with his skill and might,
who'd broke a spear on me, that I
myself had seen the splinters fly.
To each of these a golden band
was gladly given from my hand.

904   I rested well when all had gone.
I left the hostel with the dawn
and rode to Mistelbach to joust
and serve my lady sweet with lust.
Many had come to share the sport
of which I'll tell you now in short:
they broke eleven lances then
on me and I broke only ten.

905   Eleven knights with joy and pride
received the rings which I supplied,
for they were happy to have earned
the prize for which they all had yearned.
I stopped off at the inn at last
and, just as soon as night was passed,
from Mistelbach rode on again
with many good and sturdy men.

906   Two hundred knights were in the crowd
that rode with me, and most were proud;
one saw it in the gear they had
and in that they were richly clad.
But I was just as proud as they
as I rode gaily on the way
to Feldsberg. At the journey's end
the host received me as a friend.

907   Sir Kadolt von Feldsberg was his name;
from all this man received acclaim,
and rightly for his honesty.
The worthy noble rode toward me
with forty knights with trappings which
looked very fine. Their clothes were rich,
well-cut and masterfully made.
It was a splendid cavalcade.

908   I was welcomed by him there
much better than I've been elsewhere
at times. He was a courteous knight
and asked in language most polite
that I should come and be his guest.
"The queen must grant me this request
and stay with me and eat my bread.
No one could want her more," he said.

909   I sent word to the honest man
and asked that he give up the plan.
Were I to stay with anyone,
I said, I surely wouldn't shun
his house. He shouldn't take offense
but I must bear my own expense
and only take what I had bought
and not a single thing for nought.

910   He spoke, "Stay with us, lady, do.
I'd like to introduce to you
some noble ladies, fair and gay,
well-bred and nice in every way.
They want to see you, that I know,
and I intend to use them so
that to my suit you will give ear
and come, to please the ladies here."

911   I answered him, "I'd like to see
the ladies all if it might be
that I may do so and decline
to let you care for me and mine.
Please tell me what you think of this."
The knight was sad that I'd dismiss
the invitation he had sent.
Then to the hostelry we went.

917   At once I asked someone to call
the knights and to announce to all
that I would give each one a chance
to earn a lady's loving glance.
Many a good man thereupon
began to put his armor on.
I did so too and soon was decked
quite nobly, as one might expect.

918   The noise resounded all about
the town of people coming out.
At once we rode into a field
to serve the ladies with spear and shield.
The service there of some was brief
and only brought the knights to grief
but other men were glad with gain.
The service of ladies brings joy or pain.

919   Then on the field appeared a bold
and worthy man who, as was told,
with knightly deeds and knightly ways
had often won both prize and praise
wherever nobles came to serve.
He did so well as to deserve
from ladies thanks in any case;
from some he got a fond embrace.

920   Sir Siegfried Weise, so the knight
was called, was one who knew no fright
and never had a timid thought:
a good man, he, who feared for nought.
Where there was striving for a prize
he earned the thanks that none despise.
With knightly skill in many a test
he won the honor he possessed.

921   With gilded crest the noble came
onto the field to spread his fame.
The knight, renowned throughout the land,
then took a heavy spear in hand
with which he wished to joust. I tied
my helmet and was set to ride.
We spurred our horses and began
the course, I and this famous man.

922   The charge we ran was very long.
Sir Siegfried Weise, who was strong,
desired to knock me from my horse;
I had the same in mind, of course.
But still the joust was ridden well
and so that neither of us fell
although we brushed while riding fast
and broke our shields as we rushed past.

923   The joust was made so close that we
struck shield on shield and knee on knee
in riding by each other so.
Both knees were badly bruised, I know,
and both the shields were split in two.
The splinters from the lances flew
and in the collar of this lord
as well as mine wide holes were bored.

926   Thereafter I used up a score
of spears with skill and then one more.
The joust with which I broke this one,
though it was beautifully done,
brought pain and harm. I'll tell you how.
It was a pretty joust, I vow,
yet I'd been happy with a miss;
now listen, what occurred was this.

927   I'd taken a heavy weapon from
a youthful squire when I saw come
Sir Ruprecht von Purstendorf, riding hard;
he almost caught me off my guard.
I charged him, and my spear tip smote
right through his collar to his throat;
it passed through shield and mail and all.
The knight could not avoid a fall.

928   He landed far behind his steed.
At once his wound began to bleed
so that the grass about was red;
they thought at first that he was dead.
This issue caused me deepest woe.
I sadly left the field to go
into the hostel. I was filled
with grief for him I'd nearly killed.

929   But he was strong and didn't die.
The morning after, just as I
was all prepared to ride away,
a message asked that I would stay.
It came from Sir Kadolt, the host
of Feldsberg, who loved honor most.
He asked that I would visit there
his wife and many a lady fair.

930   I spoke, "This I shall gladly do
for him and for the ladies too.
I'll come to him to hear a mass
and meet the ladies as we pass."
The messenger was happy when
I told him this; he hastened then
to tell the host that I'd appear,
which all the ladies were glad to hear.

931　　At once the noble donned his best
　　　for me and was with splendor dressed.
　　　I also put some fine clothes on
　　　and rode lightheartedly thereon
　　　up to the castle where I got
　　　a friendly welcome on the spot.
　　　I thanked them warmly at our meeting
　　　and gladly heard their cordial greeting.

932　　The host received me as a friend.
　　　His wife then started to descend
　　　a stairway with the ladies all.
　　　Their trains with every step would fall
　　　down a stair before my gaze.
　　　Their fair appearance, gentle ways,
　　　and, more than these, each lovely glance
　　　soon made my heart begin to dance.

933　　I saw them coming toward me thus;
　　　to wait would not be courteous
　　　so I approached with manner mild
　　　but gay, and all the ladies smiled
　　　that I should walk so merrily
　　　with pretty women's clothes on me
　　　and lovely braids down to my hips.
　　　I met a lot of laughing lips.

934　　The wife spoke up with spritely mien,
　　　"I welcome you, my Lady Queen."
　　　I bowed politely as I heard;
　　　the others came to add a word.
　　　I offered one of them a kiss
　　　and she turned rosy red at this;
　　　I kissed another standing by
　　　who blushed, for she was also shy.

935　　When all the greetings had been said
　　　the mistress of the castle led
　　　me in a chapel, finely done;
　　　at once a service was begun
　　　and God was glorified in song.
　　　Around me was a female throng
　　　and I'll confess, the truth to tell,
　　　that God was then not served so well.

936 I was almost bound by cords of love
and by the tender glances of
a pair of shining eyes I saw.
That I escaped and could withdraw
was due alone to faithfulness.
If any woman could suppress
my constant loyalty, I swear
't would be a certain lady there.

937 Her beauty and her charm broke through
my wondering eyes before I knew
and fell into my heart. It skips
whene'er I think of the rose-red lips
which I saw laughing then at me
and which had spoken so pleasantly.
They would have stolen all my sense
were constancy not my defense.

938 For while I looked with heart aglow
my constancy addressed me so,
"How can this be? What now? What now?
For whom will you renounce your vow
to the lady you have loved so long,
who's never done you any wrong?
Away with this! He who permits
such feelings must have lost his wits."

943 I thus continued, lost in thought
and unperceiving. So distraught
can those become who fix their mind
on women. I was deaf and blind,
to all around as much as dead
until I heard the Bible read.
Another priest began it; then
I came back to myself again.

944 The ladies stood. I wished to bring
up to the front my offering
and asked the wife to lead the way.
She spoke, "Why, what would people say?
My manners would be rather mean
were I to go before a queen.
It wouldn't do my honor good;
you must not think I ever would."

945 So I went first at her request
and soon was followed by the rest.
I walked with such a happy air
that one heard laughter here and there.
To go and bow and turn around
and then come back took time, I found,
moving with a lady's stride,
no longer than a hand is wide.

948 Soon afterwards the mass was o'er
and I prepared to leave once more.
The host and also his lady sweet
invited me to stay and eat.
I spoke, "I'd gladly do your will,
since you seem to wish this still,
but constancy has sworn an oath
and so I must refuse you both.

949 "I've made this journey as I vowed,"
I said, "and never have allowed
a knight or lady yet to give
a thing but she for whom I live.
She gives me all my happiness
and is my comfort in distress,
it's she who keeps my spirits high;
and, if I serve her, that is why."

951 I rode back to my hostel then
and sent the rings to all the men
who'd driven spears against my shield
and left the splinters on the field.
I counted twenty, this is true,
but I myself broke twenty-two
good lances there as it befell.
It pleased me to have done so well.

952 While at the inn I quickly ate;
and, since I wished to leave in state,
I saw that all was in good shape,
then donned a new and pretty cape.
The dress I wore was also new.
At last I asked my retinue
to ride in splendor through the town,
so they paraded up and down.

953   We reached the Thaya soon and found
a crossing to Bohemian ground.
A lovely meadow was at hand
to which I led my festive band
and had some messengers proclaim:
who for his lady would win fame
should arm himself without delay.
I donned my armor right away.

956   A lot of nobles got the word
and came, a hundred, so I heard,
in splendid dress. They raised the shout,
"Give way, my lord, watch out! Watch out!
Let every gallant knight prepare
to honor now his lady fair!"
They rode toward me with battle lust;
I too was anxious for a joust.

957   I strained just as a falcon might.
Against me rode then many a knight;
my wish to serve my lady's pride
was fairly soon well-satisfied.
Before me many knights were massed
who rode against me thick and fast
and, through bad manners, often three
at once would charge their steeds at me.

964   I'll tell you, there was many a spear
and shield and helmet lying here.
For all about this meadow land
by many a knightly rider's hand
shields and helmets were broken through;
and here and there one saw a few
brave and skillful nobles fall
who were not used to that at all.

966   Before the tourneying was o'er
up spoke the bishop's governor,
"My noble queen, you need not stay
with us but can be on your way.
Your journey's ended, well and good,
now you can travel where you would.
I'll take your horses and your men
until you want them back again."

967 As he advised I left the place
and so as not to leave a trace.
But first I gave out rings, nineteen,
and went into a wood, unseen,
and took my armor off in haste
for I had little time to waste.
I called my servants then to tell
them every one a fond farewell.

968 With stealth, to carry out my plan
I rode off with a single man;
one of the governor's was he,
the very soul of loyalty.
Von Fronhoven he was, Sir Kol,
and well could lead me to my goal,
Vienna. Almost every stone
and every street to him was known.

969 The journey there was quickly made;
I found an inn in which I stayed
three days and nights, but while I hid,
just listen well to what I did.
I had them make the battle dress
for half-a-hundred steeds, no less;
all these were masterfully done
and quite expensive, every one.

970 But while I had these things prepared
hear how my loyal servants fared.
After I'd left them all behind
my steward with his courtly mind
took my three horses and my shirts,
as well as cloaks and capes and skirts.
Soon all the woman's clothes he found
upon the horses' backs were bound.

971 From the meadow he took everything
to where some knights were gathering.
They hurried quickly toward him then
and saw my retinue. But when
they didn't see me anywhere
and all the clothes that I'd left there
upon the horses' backs were seen,
they said at once, "Where is the queen?

972   "Yes, tell us where! Where has she gone?"
      Some other knights rode up thereon.
      My steward answered them and spoke,
      "The queen has played an evil joke
      on me that will bring grief, I fear,
      for she has gone and left me here
      and where she is I do not know.
      This changes all my joy to woe.

973   "These many articles of dress,
      these horses add to my distress.
      She left them here, what shall I do
      with them? I'd like advice from you.
      'T were wrong to take all this away;
      should I just simply let it stay
      right here? Now tell me what is best.
      I'll do whatever you suggest."

974   The governor said gallantly,
      "Good youth, it seems the best to me
      to give the minstrels here with us
      these things, and not to worry thus;
      she can get new ones for the old.
      If she's as rich as we've been told
      and as one judges by her thrift,
      she won't be injured by the gift."

975   My steward answered in this wise,
      "Lord, it shall be as you advise."
      He gave the minstrels every bit,
      just as the governor saw fit.
      At once the latter undertook
      to care for those whom I forsook
      and, since I'd given my consent,
      he led them with him when he went.

976   Right after that the noblemen
      rode back to Austria again.
      They left the Thaya soon behind
      and came to Feldsberg, there to find
      a good and rightly famous host.
      If hospitality can boast
      that it bears honor one should praise
      Sir Kadolt von Feldsberg all his days.

977 The man just would not be denied.
He brought the nobles all inside
to spend the night with him and dine.
He served good food, and mead and wine
were brought as long as they remained;
thus till his death he entertained.
They were well treated by this knight
and rode away with morning light.

986 Soon they were in Vienna too.
I was delighted when I knew
for there was nought I wanted more
than to have my servants as before.
I had the hostel decorated
at once, for I was most elated
that I should see the nobles there.
We had a merry time, I swear.

987 I bade them bring around my horse.
I wished the governor, of course,
to see me in my altered state.
The courtly noble didn't wait
and, ere my horse was gotten out
to me so I could ride about,
before the inn the knight was seen.
He spoke to me, "God greet you, queen.

988 "We see God's wonders," he began,
"in you, that you are here a man
and were but four short days ago
a woman. You have altered so;
I'll never understand just how.
You were a wealthy queen and now
are just another man we've known.
To whom did you leave your realm and throne?"

989 The knights and I all laughed a bit
as always at such clever wit.
Then those who'd ridden out to me
came thronging in the hostelry.
They wished to see who'd been so bold.
Then many a tale and joke was told
to me. We passed the evening thus;
a lot of drinks were brought to us.

990 Since I had something to confide
I led the governor aside
and told him what I planned to do.
I said, "I'd be obliged to you
if you would help me and consent
to wear throughout the tournament
my coat of arms. I'll not forget
and shall be always in your debt."

991 Then spoke the high-born nobleman,
"I'll help you any way I can,
for you need never be afraid
that I'll refuse to you my aid.
I'll gladly give it to you now
and wear your coat of arms, I vow,
throughout the tourney on my steed."
I thanked him and was pleased indeed.

992 When he had given me his word
and when the other knights had heard
that he'd agreed to my request
I had no trouble with the rest
and just asked those of highest ranks.
They all assented and with thanks:
the barons, counts, and vassals then
until I had my fifty men.

994 We stayed in Vienna four more days
and passed the time in pleasant ways.
We saw some women there in truth
the sight of whom restores one's youth.
Whoever is a gallant knight
will feel, I know, his heart beat light
to see a lady and to find
that she's both beautiful and kind.

995 On Sunday all were up at dawn
and in a hurry to be gone.
Inside the city all about
were sounds of riders moving out.
We rode away as if to war
toward Korneuburg. With us we bore
a costly banner which was made,
I'll tell you how, for this parade.

114

996   The standard had been made with care.
White taffeta it was, a pair
of bars were sewn thereon (a span
in breadth they were and black) which ran
obliquely from the right and down.
My buglers, when we left the town,
were blowing as we rode along
some marching music, high and strong.

997   Behind the banner there was borne
the helmet which I'd always worn
but now it shone just like a sword,
I do not lie, and with a cord
of finest silk a fan was bound
to it. Thus was the helmet crowned
and very prettily, it seemed.
The fan was gold and brightly gleamed.

998   It all was fashioned with great pains.
To every tip were bound the vanes
of peacock feathers, skilfully
and as I wanted them to be.
The fan was wrought with many a fold,
to each were fastened leaves of gold
so that the whole was covered o'er
with shining leaflets by the score.

999   Beside the helmet was my shield.
The whitest ermine made the field
and over this was sewn in place
two sable bars from chief to base.
Upon these bars which ran across
the field was fixed a costly boss.
To hold the shield were heavy bands
made up of many silken strands.

1007   I rode to Korneuburg that day
decked in the best of knights' array.
Before the town the Kühnringe brothers
awaited me with many others.
It was a very friendly meeting
and very courteous was their greeting.
The nobles with them were polite
and received me as beseems a knight.

1009   Thereon into the town we rode
each noble went to his abode,
inviting another whom he knew
but who had made arrangements too.
I rode into my hostel then;
to hostels went the other men
where they consumed good food and wine.
Soon many a knight was feeling fine.

1010   No food was left, no wine was spurned
by them, and wax was freely burned,
one saw a lot of flaming lights.
As often is with merry knights,
they wandered here and wandered there
around the city everywhere.
Who had no torch, the truth to tell,
could see by other torches well.

1011   That evening many nobles came
to visit me. I did the same
and gladly went to hostelries
to see such merry men as these.
Thus half the night was squandered though
I would not change a thing, I know,
for there were lots of friendships made
which never after were betrayed.

1012   The other half was spent in bed,
but when the eastern sky was red
to church we hastened right away.
Many a knight had come to pray
that God would help him to succeed.
One ought to ask God's help indeed;
except for God and for his grace
none would be happy any place.

1013   When mass was over word was sent
to choose sides for the tournament.
This soon was done as it should be,
and all divided equally.
Two-hundred-fifty knights had come
because their hearts were venturesome
and since it was their ladies' will.
They wished to demonstrate their skill.

1015   Without delay they all began
to arm themselves, each gallant man.
It did not take me long to don
my shoulder armor and put on
that for my legs. How bright they were!
'T was then I saw my messenger.
This pleased me in my inmost heart
but he soon caused me many a smart.

1016   When I beheld him waiting thus
I bade my squires depart from us
and, free of other ears and eyes,
addressed the courier in this wise,
"My messenger, to me so dear,
I offer you a welcome here.
What is the story that you bring
and did she send me anything?"

1017   He sighed with sorrow then and said
no word but stood with lowered head.
I spoke to him, "How's this? What meant
the sigh? What has the lady sent
to me? Why are you acting so?
You've never looked so filled with woe.
My joys are gone and I'm accursed;
your silence makes me fear the worst."

1018   He spoke, "I'll tell you with regret,
my lord, what I would fain forget;
't would make me happy, it is true.
The message I'm to bring to you
is so distressing, I am sure,
that if your lifetime should endure
a thousand years you'd still bewail
what you'll discover in my tale.

1019   "Your lady wishes me to state,
for you she feels nought else but hate
and will not see you any more.
She says, you well deserve this for
disloyalty of every kind,
and that she very soon will find
a way to punish what you've done.
She told me this, the virtuous one.

1021   "She told me why her wrath is such
and how you angered her so much.
She said, the news was given her
as really true that you prefer
to serve another lady now,
and this was stated as a vow;
she knows your lack of constancy.
Thus spoke your lady fair to me."

1023   I cried, "Alas, the dreadful pain
which I shall always bear in vain
within my heart until I die:
to choose a lady fair whom I
desire and love with faithfulness
and have her cause me such distress.
I've only grief, my joy has fled;
I wish to God that I were dead!

1024   "Or that I never had been born!
How did I earn her wrath and scorn
and, being constant, lose her favor,
with loyalty that would not waver?
How could my fortune be so bad!
God knows indeed I never had
disloyal thoughts and was not peeved
whatever treatment I received."

1027   I wept there as a child who fears
and I was nearly blind with tears;
I wrung my hands the while I wept.
My aching heart could not accept
this sorrow and with pain was racked.
In every joint my members cracked
as one breaks sticks to feed a flame.
My grief was not a childish game.

1028   While I was weeping, filled with gloom,
the governor came in the room
and spoke, "What can this be? What's this?"
He turned around then to dismiss
the page. "Go out," he said quite grim
and closed the door right after him.
"Now," spoke the knight so brave and strong,
"just tell me who has done you wrong."

1030   That he should speak so kindly then
made all my grief come back again
so that my tears flowed as before.
I cried, "Alas, forevermore.
I sorrow that I cannot say
to any why I grieve this way.
The cause of all the pain I feel
is something I may not reveal."

1031   But when the faithful man had seen
and heard my grief and knew how keen
the torment was, he sorrowed too
and, by my truth, I say to you,
soon joined in my lament and cried
as if his father dear had died
though why he wept he did not know;
a strange occurrence but it's so.

1032   And, as I saw him weeping there,
within my breast the pain and care
once more became so great I bowed
my head with woe and cried aloud,
"Alas that I have life and breath,
may God in mercy give me death!
From this sad world would I depart."
I longed for death with all my heart.

1033   While we displayed such anguish here
who but Sir Heinrich should appear.
Von Wasserberg, as he was named,
for chivalry was widely famed
and was my sister's husband. He
exclaimed, "See here, what might this be?
And who has ventured to provoke
such woe in you?" With wrath he spoke.

1034   "In truth I'd like to hear your tale.
This is a most unknightly wail,
for you lament as loud and wild
as any orphaned beggar child
or any woman who's afraid.
Is this the way a knight is made?
No. Whatever is amiss
you ought to be ashamed of this."

1035   "Sir Heinrich," said the governor,
"Sir Ulrich's suffering is more
than I have ever seen or heard
but I don't know what has occurred.
It's something he will not relate
although his trouble is so great
it pains me too. I cannot guess
what is the cause of such distress."

1036   Sir Heinrich was a forthright man.
"Sir Governor," he thus began,
you ought to leave us two alone
and what it is that makes him groan
and weep he'll surely have to share
for I shall ever help him bear
his sad misfortune faithfully.
To aid my friend is joy to me."

1037   The governor soon went away.
Sir Heinrich then without delay
made sure the door was firmly tied
and angrily began to chide,
"This isn't how you ought to act.
We should be happy, that's a fact,
because of all the praise you've won
with knightly deeds that you have done."

1039   I spoke and answered thus the knight,
"My heart will never more be light,
in this you can believe your ears.
Were I to live a thousand years
I would not cease to sorrow still.
Though you may think it good or ill
I'll grieve because of what befell
but what it was I cannot tell."

1041   He said as soon as I was through,
"I know what has befallen you.
Listen, I'll tell you what is wrong:
the lady you have served so long
and faithfully, my worthy lord,
to gain a lover's fair reward,
who has your service and your vow
and promised much to you till now

120

1042   her favor has denied at last.
        This must be why you're so downcast
        and why one hears these cries of woe.
        You must admit that this is so."
        At once when he said this the blood
        came from my mouth, in truth a flood
        out of my nose began to race
        till it had reddened all my face.

1043   As soon as he beheld me bleed
        the courtly man cried out indeed,
        "Dear God, I offer thanks to Thee
        that Thou permittest me to see
        before my death a gallant man
        of whom in very truth I can
        maintain, he loved without deceit
        or wavering his lady sweet."

1044   He knelt before me as I bled
        and raised his hands above his head
        and thankfully these words confessed,
        "In seeing it my soul is blessed!
        I'm grateful just to know of this,
        it fills my heart with sweetest bliss
        to make me happy all my days.
        I'll always think of this with praise."

1052   Again my sobbing made me weak.
        I started wretchedly to speak,
        "I must give up the tournament.
        One can not tourney and lament;
        in knightly games one can't be sad,
        what one does then will turn out bad.
        To serve a lady well a knight
        must joust but do so with delight."

1054   The honor-loving honest man
        laughed at my statement and began,
        "All this has been decided on,
        your armor you will have to don.
        Though it be joy or more distress
        you'll get into your battle dress."
        He put it on me hastily
        but got no word of thanks from me.

121

1055   He placed my helmet on me last,
then with his hands he tied it fast
and led me out of there with force
to where I found, all decked, my horse.
I mounted with my grief unhealed,
at once he gave to me my shield
and so with sorrow and belated
I rode to where the others waited.

1056   They waited right before the inn,
with shining trappings, to begin.
Their battle dress too gleamed and glowed
as to the jousting field we rode.
I saw Sir Hadmar von Kühnringe then
surrounded by a troop of men
and also saw Sir Heinrich, his brother,
who was the center of another.

1057   While helmets onto heads were tied
we formed the groups with which we'd ride.
I took a sturdy spear in hand
and rode away then from our band.
I came forth all alone indeed
and then began to spur my steed
to race as fast as he could go.
I charged Sir Hadmar's forces so.

1058   And when I reached the troop I broke
my spear off with a skilful stroke;
it shattered well though it was large.
I did not slow my rapid charge
but rode their spears and shields in two.
Sir Hadmar's men did not pursue,
for courteously he cried, "Don't stay
him now, just let him ride away."

1062   I rode as fast as I could spur
back to where my comrades were
and spoke, "Let's start the tournament;
I got away by their consent.
Were I to splinter thirty spears
against them, they, so it appears,
would let me keep escaping thus.
I think, because they're courteous."

1063 At once I took another lance.
We saw Sir Hadmar's troop advance
toward us and at a rapid pace.
I turned my men about to face
the strong attack the noble led;
he was both skilled and spirited.
We charged the foe just as one should,
riding as closely as we could.

1064 And when the other troop was nigh
I spurred my charger so that I
was moving very swiftly when
I struck the first of Hadmar's men.
On him I broke my spear in two,
plunged in the troop and then crashed through.
My knights all followed after me
and struck them hard and skilfully.

1065 When we broke through his squadron so
Hadmar von Kühnringe wasn't slow
to get his troop in shape once more.
He caught three of my men before
they ever got their horses turned;
he was a master, as they learned.
He knew a lot and was precise
and often gave some good advice.

1066 But we surrounded him and might
have captured Hadmar when a knight
(his brother Heinrich) led a raid
against us, coming to his aid.
Sir Heinrich's troop rode well and fast
and rammed our horses as they passed.
One heard their lances loudly crack
and saw them slowly force us back.

1067 As we by foes were ringed about
a squadron came to help us out:
it was Sir Wolfger with his band.
He galloped up with spear in hand.
The valiant knight had taken care
to catch the foe quite unaware;
the charge was carried out with skill,
for Hadmar this meant only ill.

1068   There were no others who could ride
to help; two troops on either side,
no more, were in the tournament.
The honor-loving nobles spent
their strength and lances so that they
won glory and renown that day.
But it was clearly true that none
gained easily the fame he won.

1070   Many a man in these affrays
through gallant exploits won high praise.
Low-minded nobles were not there
to strive; it's like that everywhere.
The true knight seeks an honored name
to others it is all the same
if they have ease and property.
The difference isn't hard to see.

1071   "Crash! Bang!" until the day was o'er
rode Lengenbach, the governor.
Sir Wolfger von Gors was tireless here
and on the foe broke many a spear,
he never stopped throughout the fight.
Sir Dietmar von Liechtenstein, a knight
who's always striving to excel,
was one who tourneyed very well.

1072   Sir Heinrich von Wasserberg had done
that day as much as anyone;
von Kiowe, who was very stout,
was praised by everyone about;
Sir Ulrich von Steutz displayed such skill
that people talk about it still;
and what the knight, von Ottenstein,
did to the enemy was fine.

1073   Sir Engelschalk used many a lance
and risked his honor on pure chance;
this Lord of Königsbrunnen threw
it often on the scales, it's true,
one owes him praise for recklessness.
Von Rebstock strove and with success
for fame and his desire was such,
he thought no labor was too much.

1074   Were I to name you all the men
whose exploits were outstanding then,
who strove and honor there would find,
and name all those of gallant mind,
and tell how one crashed through the foe,
how that man's lance was splintered so,
how he was bold, and he was strong,
you'd think my story much too long.

1075   You've heard a lot of tourneying
so I'll not add a single thing
to what I've told except to say
that I used up nine spears that day.
In brief, it's this I want to tell,
that all the sturdy knights did well
and each man strove with every limb;
these sought to gain renown for him.

1076   The darkness stopped the tournament
and from the field at last we went
back to the inns with manly pride.
I rode to mine and found inside
the knights I'd taken prisoner.
I let them go just as they were,
without a loss, through courtesy.
They all expressed their thanks to me.

1077   In Korneuburg we spent the night,
and with the early morning light
all travelled home with spirits high.
I rode from there with many a sigh.
When he beheld my lowered head
the loyal messenger then said,
"It causes me much pain and woe
when I must see you sorrow so."

1078   I spoke to him, "Dear friend, now say,
how could my heart again be gay,
how could I hope for happiness?
My lady grants me no success,
which means that I shall never more
be happy-hearted as before.
My joyful spirit now is gone
and I can only sorrow on."

1079   The youth replied, "Lord, I believe
that it will do no good to grieve;
do not despair of pleasure now.
Of course, I cannot tell you how
your lady actually may feel;
it's possible her wrath is real
but maybe it's a test for you.
These are things that women do.

1080   "I'd like to recommend a plan
with which I'll help you all I can:
why don't I see if I can find
if she's unfavorably inclined
or whether this is just a test.
Before I'll see you so distressed
I'll try it once again indeed.
God grant my efforts may succeed."

1081   "Page, you've never failed me yet
and I'll be always in your debt.
I say, the plan you recommend
is one which pleases me no end.
It's really more than I dared ask
but you yourself assume the task
of helping me. May God confer
rich blessings on you, messenger."

1088   The messenger departed then
and I rode onward, sad again,
until at last I came to where
I found a lot of loving care,
to my sweet wife. She couldn't be
in any way more dear to me
although I'm in the service of
another, who's my lady love.

1090   But hear what happened to the squire:
he needs what help he can acquire
from luck and from a gracious fate.
When he arrived at her estate
she laughed because he looked so grim
but welcomed and then questioned him,
"Now tell me what your lord has done.
Say, am I still his chosen one?"

1091

"Yes, lady, though you be unkind
to him he has so fixed his mind
that no one else can be so dear,
not even life itself, I fear.
He loves you more than any thing
and serves you with no wavering.
I'll take an oath and swear to this
by all my hope of heaven's bliss."

1097

She spoke, "I grant him my esteem
and tell you truly, though I seem
to show disfavor, it's not so;
but this is what you need to know:
that which he wishes in return
for service he can never earn.
He should not think this hate or spite,
the same is true of any knight.

1102

"Ride to your master now and say
what I told you. If there's a way
I'd like to meet him secretly,
could it be managed so that he
might take such care and not expose
us when he comes and when he goes
that none will know the guest I've had.
If this can be then I'll be glad.

1103

"My counsel, since he's venturesome,
is this: as lepers you must come
on Sunday morning (don't be late)
and join the lepers by the gate.
You'll knock as soon as you arrive
and very shortly I'll contrive
to send a maid; what she directs,
so do it that no one suspects.

1104

"You must tell him another thing:
he should not come here wondering
if I shall let him in my bed;
he must not be so far misled.
That I'll be glad to see him here
does not mean (you must make this clear)
that he will gain the love he's sought.
This prospect isn't worth a thought.

127

1105 "I only let him come to me
because you've often said that he
has served me well his lifetime through.
Now mark what I shall say to you.
I want him as a secret guest
so I can make this one request:
that he will let this service end.
I ask this truly as a friend."

1106 "I'll tell him, lady, your desire
and know he'll do as you require.
He'll come as quickly as he can:
this news will make a happy man.
My lord will surely not decline
but come at once, as you design,
in clothing like the lepers wear—
just as you wish him, he'll be there."

1107 The messenger departed then
and rode to where I just had been;
since I'd already left the place
he followed at a hurried pace.
He galloped onward night and day
and seldom rested on the way;
he proved himself a friend of mine.
He found me there at Liechtenstein.

1109 The moment that I saw him ride
so hastily toward me I cried
with joy, "Here comes the page at last;
now I'll no longer be downcast.
Perhaps he has good news to tell
(no other does it near so well)
and it may be that he'll impart
that which will ease my aching heart."

1110 I rode to him—I couldn't wait
but had to hear what he'd relate—
and said, "You're welcome, messenger,
and more so than you ever were.
I must admit in very truth,
I'm really glad to see you, youth.
I hope to God that you'll report
good tidings from the lady's court."

1114
"The lady wishes me to say,
she'd like to see you right away
but you must meet her secretly.
On Sunday it's supposed to be
and early, ere the sun is high.
Before the gate some ruins lie
and you're to come there in disguise—
thus says your lady sweet and wise.

1115
"You must appear in ragged dress
such as a leper might possess
and what her courier may direct,
that carry out; be circumspect
so no one guesses you're a knight.
Thus speaks the lady fair and bright:
if you are smart there'll be no shame
for you, and she will get no blame.

1116
"And you should know what else she said:
you must not come if you're misled;
no matter how you beg or sigh
she's never going to let you lie
with her. That simply may not be
but just the same she'd like to see
you. She'd enjoy a friendly chat.
The charming lady told me that."

1120
"I must get ready for the ride
and hope that God is on my side.
I'll see if I can make it there;
the days are long, the weather's fair,
one travels far from sun to sun.
I think perhaps it can be done
and I can get there when she wanted.
At least my spirit is undaunted.

1121
"We'll take with us a single groom,
a man who's capable, on whom
I can depend, who'll not discuss
the trip. There'll be just three of us.
Six horses, known for strength and speed,
shall go along. If there is need
I'll race them till they all are dead,
to be there Sunday, as she said."

The Adventure of How Sir Ulrich Came as a Leper to His Lady and of How He Saw Her

1124   'T was Friday night so we stayed on
        but Saturday morning, just at dawn,
        we three set out to make the trip.
        I took great care that none let slip
        where we were travelling or why
        and was resolved to show that I
        could manage so that not a soul
        might ever guess the journey's goal.

1125   On my knightly word I vow
        I rode that Saturday somehow
        one-hundred-sixty miles and more.
        When that day's trip at last was o'er
        I was so tired. Along the way
        I lost two horses, dead they lay
        beside the road. I dared not wait
        and did not think their loss too great.

1126   'T was in the town where we arrived
        so late that night that I contrived
        to get some clothing, poor and torn,
        and beggar's bowls. On Sunday morn
        we donned the rags with many a curse,
        they couldn't possibly be worse.
        Instead of swords we took some knives,
        which we might need to save our lives.

1127   On Sunday morning early we
        rode eight miles further. Carefully
        I hid the groom and horses, then
        the page and I went on again
        for seven miles until we stood
        before a castle. There the good
        and gracious lady chiefly dwelt.
        I cannot tell you how I felt.

1128   We walked up closer till we found
        some wretched people all around
        who showed their poverty and need.
        There were a lot, I think, indeed
        full thirty lepers. Most of these
        had suffered much from their disease
        and some of those I saw with dread
        were very sick and nearly dead.

1129   I had to go to them and sit
        (I didn't care for this a bit
        and did it at my friend's command)
        as if I were too weak to stand.
        They greeted us, the sickly group,
        with many a gasping cough and whoop,
        and so diseased I could not bear
        to look, but still I joined them there.

1130   While we were seated they began
        to ask us questions, every man
        desired to know from whence we'd come.
        I found this query troublesome.
        I spoke, "We come from no place near,
        we both are total strangers here
        and want has brought us to this spot
        to see if they are kind or not."

1131   One said to us, "You couldn't pick
        a better time; the lady's sick
        who is the mistress of the place,
        and so they purchase heaven's grace
        by bringing us the food we crave.
        Before you came a maiden gave
        us bread and even wine. For this
        I pray she gains eternal bliss."

1133   Then, going from the lepers, we
        approached a little balcony,
        before which hung a heavy shade;
        of costly fabric this was made.
        They often hang such curtains to
        keep light and wind from coming through.
        This one was sturdy and was fast;
        through it no breezes ever passed.

1134
I took my bowl out (in the light
it looked a bit too clean and bright)
and knocked with it so loud that all
could hear who then were in the hall.
As soon as I had knocked I stood
and begged as loudly as I could
that I might get a piece of bread,
for many days I'd not been fed.

1135
A maiden, when she heard my plea,
looked down at once from the balcony
to find out who had made the fuss
and saw there were just two of us.
She quickly closed the shade and went
to tell her lady of my lament
and that below were two strange men.
The lady sent her to us then.

1138
She came up close and spoke quite low
to us, "You two must let me know
just who and what you are; now say!
I must find out and right away
for I'm supposed to only pause
a moment. Did you come because
my noble lady sent for you?
Make sure that what you tell is true."

1139
I spoke thus to the pretty maid,
"My lady, you shall be obeyed.
For I am here at her command;
know this, that I am he whose hand
has always been at her employ,
and I am he whose only joy
may come from her. She can depend
on me to serve her till the end."

1141
"The lady waits for my return.
I'll go to her and she shall learn
that you are here because she sent
for you. With that she'll be content.
I'll quickly come back here again
and give instructions to you then
of what she wants of you today."
With that the maiden went away

1142   to find at once the lady fair
and let her know that I was there.
She told her all and did not hide
a thing. The lady thus replied,
"I'm very pleased indeed to hear
of his arrival. Go, my dear,
and tell him what I said, in sum,
that I am glad that he has come.

1144   "He must return this evening. I
shall send a message telling why
I bade him come, and he shall find
just what it is I have in mind.
He'll then know everything he should.
But you must take him something good
to eat: some chicken, bread, and wine;
give him God's greeting too, and mine."

1145   The maiden, when she knew her will,
returned and found me waiting still.
She and another girl now bore
what she'd been told to bring and more.
When I saw she had company,
I set my bowl some yards from me
and spoke, "My lady, fill it quick
and go for I am very sick."

1146   At that the second maid stopped dead
but she I knew came near and said,
"I'll take whatever fate decrees
and not be scared by your disease.
My worthy lady sends to you
a welcome and God's greeting too.
She says, she'll gladly see the one
who serves her, when this can be done.

1148   "Go now, and when the sun has set
come back up here and I shall let
you hear whatever she may tell
to me. I know she likes you well.
Of this at least you can be sure,
that of a truth my lady pure
such favor ne'er before has shown."
And then she left me there alone.

1149

I carried off, when she had gone,
the food and drink to pass it on
to lepers who were waiting there.
I spoke, "I've got enough to share
with you. May God this lady bless
with many years of happiness.
She's given more than I shall need;
I'll gladly share with you indeed."

1151

We all sat down to form a ring
and placed inside it everything
that had been given by the maid.
The hands I saw were so decayed
they looked—I dare not tell you how;
it's more than manners will allow.
Upon my honor, I contend,
my hair in horror stood on end.

1152

A foul disease was there disclosed.
Some fingers were as decomposed,
the flesh and bones as foul and rotten
as those of bodies long forgotten
and buried for a hundred days.
It's true, and not an idle phrase:
no dog could have such evil breath;
already they belonged to death.

1153

And with these sick I had to eat.
How much I wanted to retreat
and never share with them a meal
but I was forced to stay, conceal
my dread, and carefully preserve
the name of her I wished to serve,
for if I had refused to stay
they would have wondered right away.

1160

To pass the time I walked to town
and begged until the sun went down
and lit the mountain with its glow.
'T was nearly evening, time to go
back to the castle gate once more.
I took my place there as before
among the others. Cordially
the many lepers greeted me.

1162   When I'd been sitting there a while
the maiden came and led a file
of servants bearing food and wine.
There was enough for all to dine.
She spoke to me, "You must arise
and go. Now do as I advise.
Be back again with morning light
and take especial care tonight."

1163   I spoke, "Why did my lady dear
command my strange existence here
if I am not to talk with her?"
The maiden spoke, "This can't occur
before tomorrow night. Her plan
is this: to see you when she can
and certainly before you're gone.
Just see that no one catches on."

1166   I hurried from the castle ground
into a distant field. I found
some grain there, growing thick and high,
in which we hid from every eye
(the messenger was there as well).
The field of grain was our hotel
and, I assure you, it was bad.
That was a dreary night we had.

1167   For just as soon as day was done
and when the night had scarce begun
a stormy wind swept o'er the grain
and brought with it a driving rain.
'T was most unpleasant in the field,
against the rain my only shield
a shabby robe and scanty cloak:
as shelter both were just a joke.

1168   From wet and cold I almost died,
but I had other ills beside.
Although I should leave something out
I really ought not talk about—
the unnamed insects caused me grief
the whole night long without relief,
they didn't give me any rest.
That night I boarded many a guest.

1170   A night like this I'd never spent
and, had I not such fond intent
that night to help me to endure
all this, I would have died, I'm sure.
Good thoughts we can't have too much of
and better yet are thoughts of love.
Who has these with him in distress
will get much help from happiness.

1171   The morning sun came up at last.
Then through the fields I quickly passed
and stood before the castle gate.
I knocked thereon and asked with great
concern if I perhaps could get
some clothes, since all I had were wet
and I was cold. I begged for aid;
once more I saw the pretty maid.

1172   A lot of food and drink she brought.
"My lady wishes," so I thought,
"that I get sick and perish here."
At once the maiden hurried near
and said, "Last night I wondered whether
you'd found a shelter from the weather.
You look as though you'd had no bed,
nor even roof above your head."

1173   I said, "I've suffered misery.
The cold was most the death of me,
and other things tormented us
that I should really not discuss.
But this and even more I'll bear
and I'll be paid for it whene'er
the lady takes me as her knight.
I live in hope of such delight."

1174   She spoke, "Sit down and eat your fill,
then leave the castle and the hill,
return this evening when you're due.
Upon my word I promise you
my worthy lady will not let
you wait much longer, cold and wet,
for you are soon to come to her.
Tonight this meeting shall occur."

1175   When she said this to me we parted,
her words had made me happy-hearted.
I hurried to the lepers then,
I had to eat with them again
but this I did with great distaste,
and afterwards I went in haste
down to a forest where I heard
the songs of many a little bird.

1179   I sat in the forest down below
till evening and 't was time to go.
I then got up and almost ran
in happy temper like a man
whose heart with love is all afire
and thinks she'll grant him his desire;
of course his spirits would be high.
In such a fancy there went I.

1187   I left the forest to ascend
the hill when day was at an end,
driven away by dismal night
with all its dark, mysterious might.
I climbed down in the moat a ways
and hid myself from people's gaze
with many stones. As I recall,
it really took no time at all.

1188   So too the page had hidden him;
we didn't dare to move a limb.
While we lay covered on the ground
the warden made his nightly round.
He searched the castle in and out
to see no strangers were about
and that no one was hiding there.
He carefully looked everywhere.

1189   While he displayed such energy,
just hear what happend next to me.
That rascal bade his comrades stay
and walked right straight to where I lay;
he came as close as he could get
and pissed till I was soaking wet.
I couldn't move or do a thing—
a quite uncommon happening.

1190   With this he went in through the gate
while there I lay in this sad state
and suffered both distress and shame.
Out from the balcony there came
a light. I climbed up from the moat
and quickly doffed the beggar's coat
which I had worn as a disguise
and hid it from the watchman's eyes.

1191   I stole to the balcony and found
a loop of bedding, tightly bound.
At once I stepped into the band,
my comrade lent a helping hand
as from below he gave a shove;
my spirit hastened to my love
while tender hands drew up the sheet,
and so I rose — for several feet.

1192   It happened thus: as soon as I
was lifted from the ground so high
that my companion could bestow
no more assistance from below,
the ladies found they couldn't haul
me up. I dangled by the wall,
annoyed that they should pull in vain.
This also caused the ladies pain.

1193   They let me down to rest and then
they quickly pulled me up again,
right to the place I was before.
They couldn't move me anymore,
not upward, by a single hair.
By all my courtliness I swear
both they and I were in distress.
Three times they tried without success

1194   The third time down I knew indeed
this method never would succeed.
I left the bedding in a rage
and hurriedly addressed the page.
I spoke, "Good friend, I'm sure you are
less heavy than I am by far.
Step in, we'll find out if they can
lift up a smaller, lighter man."

1195   As soon as he was seated there
I lifted him into the air,
the ladies pulled him up with ease,
and I was happy as you please.
He came into their room like this
and then was greeted with a kiss.
My aunt mistook the page for me;
she was embarrassed as could be.

1196   He saw that he'd been kissed instead
of me and did not lose his head,
but quickly let the bedding fall;
't was this I wanted most of all.
It surely wasn't long until
I sat therein with all good will.
My spirit stoutly pulled with those
above as steadily I rose.

1197   This time I reached with no more slips
the balcony. My aunt's red lips
were pressed with tenderness on mine.
The charming lady made a sign
for me to follow, and we went
into a room and there she lent
to me a robe of baldaquin
that I could see my lady in.

1198   Therewith I entered thus belated
the room in which my lady waited;
she sat upon a rich divan.
The sweet and lovely one began
with greatest courtesy to greet
me while I yet approached her seat.
She bade me welcome to the place.
I answered, "Lady, grant me grace."

1199   Let me describe how she was clad.
A snow-white blouse the lady had
put on—'t was delicate and neat—
and over this my lovely sweet
displayed a scarlet garment such
that one could never praise too much:
all trimmed in ermine; till that night
I never saw a fur so white.

1204 The lady sat in front of me
and I am sure I'll never see
a lovelier beneath the sun.
I knelt before the charming one
and spoke, "My lady, by your truth,
by your celebrated youth,
by your pure and noble mind,
I pray, be good to me and kind.

1205 "Lady, you're my chief delight,
may I be favored in your sight,
may your compassion take my part.
Consider the longing of my heart
which constant love for you inspired.
Consider that I have not desired
a thing more beautiful than you,
a lovelier I never knew.

1206 "You're dearer far than all that I
have ever seen. If I could lie
with you tonight then I'd possess
all that I've dreamed of happiness.
My life will gain by your assent
a lofty spirit and content
more and more until it ends.
It's you on whom my joy depends."

1207 Then spoke the lady sweet and kind,
"It never should have crossed your mind
that I would let you lie with me.
You should not come with such a plea,
nor let a prayer like this be heard,
for I shall tell you on my word
and truly that you will not sway
me—now—no matter what you say.

1209 "Your many valiant deeds have brought
to you such fame a woman ought
to grant you gladly this request;
and, could I do as you suggest,
I would. But still you should be proud
and honored that I have allowed
you in my room. This is a lot
and more than any other got.

1210 "You see, my husband and my lord
would never want me to reward
another so or give my love.
Were I not checked by God above
or by my honor, he would guard
me closely though this would be hard.
Indeed a watch would be in vain
had I not honor to maintain.

1211 "My pure intent does him more good
than any watching ever would.
That I should risk my honor still
and also risk my lord's good will
is only done to honor you.
And, if some people ever knew
of this, my honor would disappear.
You owe me thanks that you are here."

1212 "I thank you. I am in your debt
and, lady, I shall ne'er forget
what you have done and do for me.
For I've no doubt your sympathy
will cause you, blessed lady fair,
to drive away my pain and care
by granting me tonight love's bliss,
right here and now. I'm sure of this."

1213 She spoke to me, "If what you prize
is my esteem, it's most unwise
to ask for what could harm my name
although I tell you, what you claim
can simply not be granted now.
If you persist you'll lose, I vow,
what favor you have won. It's so."
I got up startled by this blow

1214 and quickly went to where I'd seen
my aunt and asked, "What can this mean?
If I have come up here in vain
I haven't won a thing but pain.
I can't believe her so unkind;
it must not be what she designed
for she's not acting as she ought.
The lady has to give this thought."

1216 My aunt spoke up, "It's what she meant;
I know for sure, her sole intent
was what she said and nothing more,
that's all you were invited for.
There's something else which I should say:
she had so many of us stay
in case you thought of using force,
to which men sometimes have recourse.

1217 "I know it's true and must declare,
if you so much as touch a hair
against her will she'll not receive
you ever after (this believe),
and even should you not succeed.
One thing I've heard her say indeed:
if in her service you'll not waver
she yet may grant to you this favor."

1218 "I'll not contend with her a bit
against her will but, I admit,
it's just because I know those here
would very quickly interfere.
If there weren't such a lot of you
I'd wrestle her. When we were through
she'd grant the prize of victory.
I'll tell you, this is what would be."

1219 "Nephew, hear me and obey.
I know she likes you anyway;
just do now as she wants, and I
am rather sure that you will lie
with her quite soon. For you will find
the lady really is so kind
and is so very feminine
that pretty soon you're bound to win."

1221 I went back to the lady sweet
and said, "Dear lady, I entreat
you by the grace and loveliness
which through God's mercy you possess,
do not permit that we should part
like this. They praise your tender heart:
reveal it here to me, and so
that I may be happy ere I go.

1224

"Mistress, greatest joy I know,
mistress, you my pleasure's glow,
mistress of my heart and soul,
mistress of my every goal.
mistress over every stone
I have and all I'll ever own,
mistress, only you can give
content, for you alone I live.

1225

"You it is who must preserve
my happiness. It's you I'll serve
with faithfulness until the last.
And should a thousand years go past
my service always would endure,
my loyalty would be as sure.
That's why you ought to grant me bliss
in tenderness. I ask for this."

1228

Then spoke the lady pure and fair,
"I cannot listen to your prayer.
If I had planned to make love now
I'm smart enough to find somehow
a way to meet you privately.
Now listen to this word from me:
if you continue thus to prate
you're really going to win my hate.

1237

"I've told you twice; you can depend
on this, that I do not intend
to give you love, not right away.
Were you as smart as people say,
and if you valued my good will,
you'd surely keep such wishes still
through which from me you'll never gain
a thing, and which can bring you pain."

1239

Unhappily I stood up then;
I went to see my aunt again
and, when I found her, spoke dismayed,
"Aunt, once more I need your aid
and honest counsel for," I said,
"you know, I'd rather far be dead
than have her favor thus denied
and go away unsatisfied.

1243   "I'm very sure that if I choose
to stay till morning I shall lose
at once and certainly my life,
but yet with me the worthy wife
will have her good repute to mourn—
I would have better not been born.
She needs to give the matter thought
for I shall never leave for nought."

1244   Then said my aunt, "I'd better go
at once and let the lady know
that you have said you're going to wait
right here, regardless of your fate,
and don't expect to change your mind,
and that, if she is not resigned
to losing honor, she must fear,
for you intend to perish here."

1245   My aunt then left me standing there
and went to find my lady fair.
She spoke, "See, lady, what you get,
my nephew Ulrich's so upset
that he won't leave the place, it's true,
till he gets what he wants from you.
Now see, my lady, that you act
so that your honor stays intact."

1246   The lady fair and virtuous
then said, "It's bad for both of us;
you're right, for me as well as him.
Though he not fear for life and limb
he should be careful just the same
and not endanger my good name.
This certainly he should defend
and leave here quickly as a friend.

1247   "You must go back to him and say,
he doesn't need to act this way,
that he may well be light at heart.
If he'll obey me and depart
he has my word that I'll fulfill
his hopes and later do his will.
If he'll act now as I suggest
I'll gladly grant him his request.

1248   "Now tell him, had he acted right
        and had he done my will tonight
        there'd be no reason to complain,
        he'd not have had his trip in vain
        for I'd have quickly given in.
        But, if he thinks that he can win
        my love like this and can compel
        assent, then he's not thinking well."

1250   My aunt then left her and returned
        to where I waited, still concerned.
        She said, "At last you can be merry
        and all your sorrows you can bury.
        Your worries are quite needless for
        no lady ever offered more
        than she will give if you'll agree
        to follow her guidance willingly.

1253   "Dear nephew, you must be content
        and not get in an argument
        for, if you don't do what she said,
        then truly all your hopes are dead
        and you'll have nothing but regret.
        Woo her gently and you'll yet
        enjoy her love before you go.
        The gracious lady told me so."

1254   While she was talking with me thus
        my charming lady came to us
        and spoke to me just like a queen,
        "God knows that I have never seen
        a man who has so little sense.
        You'll sooner drive my favor hence
        than be successful in your suit
        by this quarrelsome dispute.

1260   "If, when you came, I'd greeted you,"
        the lady said, "as lovers do
        then I would never let you go
        away from here while feeling so.
        Obey me now, it's for the best,
        and do for once as I request.
        Get back again into the sheet,
        I'll let you down for several feet

1261
"then pull you up without delay
and greet you in another way.
When I've received you, not until,
then I'll be subject to your will,
whatever you may want with me.
I've chosen you, as you will see,
of all the knights both far and near,"
thus spoke the lady fair and dear.

1262
"Were I but sure of that, I would
do quickly what you say I should
but my offense makes me afraid.
I fear that it may be repaid
in that you'll let me down and then
will never pull me up again.
My spirit would be so forlorn
that I were better never born."

1263
The lady spoke, "If you demand
security just hold my hand,
I'll let you do it if I must.
Perhaps you're not a man to trust
since you don't trust me from your sight
although I chose you as my knight
above all others whom I knew.
As I'm a woman, this is true."

1264
"I shall, my lovely lady fair,
put soul and body in your care
and at your mercy, as is fit.
Though good or ill may come of it
I'll do whatever you propose.
Because you told me that you chose
me as your lover I shall bless
and gladly trust your tenderness."

1265
She said then, "This will serve you well.
If you will do now as I tell
you to I'll give my promise here:
You needn't have the slightest fear;
I'll do your will, whate'er it be,
and you at last may lie with me.
Your wants shall all be satisfied."
Thus spoke the lady by my side.

1266   The fair one took my hand and we
went over to the balcony
and found the bedding on the floor.
She told me to get in once more
and said, "Don't have the slightest fear;
I gladly give my promise here:
you won't leave now, it's not the end.
I've chosen you to be my friend."

1267   Though worried, I then took my seat
inside the tightly knotted sheet.
They let me down a little ways
to where they were supposed to raise
me up. My sweet continued slyly,
"God knows, I never thought so highly
of any noble in the land
as of the knight who holds my hand.

1268   "My friend," she spoke, "be welcome so.
We both are freed from care and woe
and I can now invite you in."
While speaking thus, she raised my chin
and said, "Dear one, give me a kiss."
I was so overjoyed with this
I let her hand go free and I
quite soon had cause to grieve thereby.

1269   I kissed her then as I was bid
and let her hand loose as I did;
so very swift was my descent
that, had not God in mercy lent
protection, there can be no doubt,
I surely would have tumbled out,
but I came down without a fall.
They pulled the sheets back up the wall.

1270   I sat right down in great despair.
The grief was more than I could bear
and reason fled in my distress;
I was so mad and comfortless
I cried aloud in bitter pain,
"Alas, alas, and all in vain!
Alas, that I was ever born
my hopes and honor thus to mourn!"

1271   I sprang up then so overwrought
that I had neither sense nor thought
and raced unthinking down a steep
incline to water which was deep
to drown myself in that dark lake,
which would have been a bad mistake.
My comrade followed hastily
else it had been the end of me.

1272   They'd quickly lowered him down too.
When he, so courteous and true,
heard how I cried at being spurned
my loyal friend was quite concerned.
He stayed close by me through it all;
when I was just about to fall
into the water, deep and black,
he grasped my arm and held me back.

1273   He cried out, "What do you intend
to do, my master and my friend?
It's terrible that you should try
to jump into this lake and die.
You'd lose both soul and body then
and had much better never been.
Why you're a man who's strong and brave;
is this the way you should behave?"

1274   "It has to be this way," I said,
"and truly I shall soon be dead
for here shall I give up my life
since I have lost the lovely wife
and that because of my own fault.
So it's myself I shall assault
and seek this so ignoble death.
In truth, I want no life or breath.

1277   "How sadly I have been deceived
by this sweet lady, I believed!
She said, I should have faith in her,
that such a thing would not occur,
and then she let me hold her pale
and tender hand as precious bail.
She got it back through plain deceit,
't was not a very honest feat."

1278   My comrade's voice was full of cheer:
        "My lord, this you'll be glad to hear
        (I'll tell you truly, as is right) —
        she wants you back tomorrow night.
        The charming lady, you will find,
        will then be loving and so kind
        that you will get your will with ease
        and do with her just as you please.

1279   "But here you can no longer stay,
        we must be quickly on our way,
        the dawn has come, it's getting late
        and it is dangerous to wait.
        We need to leave here while we can
        and see if your young, foolish man
        is with the horses, as expected,
        or whether he has been detected.

1280   "I truly fear that we were wrong
        in leaving him alone so long
        for anyone who sees him there
        will also soon be quite aware
        those horses must belong to you,
        and think what damage that can do.
        Unless the horses stay concealed
        the whole affair will be revealed."

1282   I spoke, "What you have said is wise
        and I shall do as you advise,
        this thought has also come to me;
        we ought to go at once and see.
        And, if we have the horses still,
        then we can come again, and will,
        to find out whether she will let
        me back into her chambers yet."

1283   Without delay we hastened then
        to where the horses once had been.
        We found them there and with the boy
        who greeted me with honest joy
        and said, "My Lord, I cannot tell
        how glad I am to see you well.
        I've suffered so from fear and dread;
        I was afraid that you were dead."

1285 Quickly spoke the courtly youth,
"Sir, you will have to know the truth.
I dare not hazard more delay
and need to tell you right away
what is the lady's real intent.
But promise first that you repent
this morning's madness, as you should;
the news is really pretty good."

1287 I said, "My friend, you'd best relate
the truth to me and simply state
the message you were told to bring;
for God's sake, don't conceal a thing,
just tell me what it was you heard.
Don't be afraid, I give my word
that I shall not fall prey once more
to madness, as I did before."

1288 "This is the message she conveys
through me to you: in twenty days
from now she wants you to return.
Hear this, you need have no concern,
the lady will receive you so
that you'll be happy when you go.
The beautiful and worthy wife
will make you happy then for life.

1289 "That which occurred to you just now
she had no choice but to allow —
I got this from your lady fair.
Among the women who were there
. . . . . [line missing] . . . . . .
You must believe she had to let
this wretched incident occur;
't would not have happened but for her.

1290 "That woman soon will travel on
and they'll be happy when she's gone.
Then you're supposed to come back here
(your lady made this very clear).
Ten days she wishes you to dwell
with her, and it's the truth I tell.
This time she'll really treat you right,
as a lady ought to treat her knight."

1292 With this, I mounted up and rode
to Liechtenstein, for there abode
my retinue. They greeted me
with joy. I thanked them readily.
They said, "We're glad your trip is done
and glad to see you, every one.
Where you had gone, we could not learn
and we are pleased at your return."

1293 I thanked them for the joy expressed
and sought a room where I could rest.
I stayed three days, then led my band
toward Austria, and in this land.
For at St. Pölten had been set
a tournament. I wished to get
there with my half-a-dozen men.
The messenger rode with me then.

1294 And as I passed along the road
my pain became a heavy load.
I spoke thus to the messenger,
"If you should want to prove you were
my friend I'd like to have you ride
no longer with us by my side
but to my lady kind and true.
I ask this favor now of you.

1295 "Find out for me just how she feels
and everything her mind reveals:
if she's an enemy or friend,
if she has plans to recommend,
how I'm to come there in disguise
and hide myself from curious eyes.
Find out these things and what's her mood.
I'll owe you deepest gratitude."

1296 "I'll go again since it's your will;
God grant that I not serve you ill
and that I find her well-inclined.
I'll gladly tell you what's her mind,
if she has blame for you or praise;
I should be back in several days.
Be gallant in the tournament
for she'll discover how it went."

1297 He quickly rode from me to where
   he found my lady sweet and fair.
   She saw him and addressed him thus,
   "I'm glad to have you here with us.
   Now tell me honestly, good youth,
   and see you don't conceal the truth,
   how is your master making out
   and what did you come to talk about?"

1298 "My lady," he replied, "I know,
   if you'd be kind enough to show
   him favor he'd not feel so badly.
   God knows, you treat him pretty sadly
   (since I'm to tell what's true and right),
   for I have never seen a knight
   who ever loved a woman more
   than he loves, though his heart is sore.

1299 "I'll tell what happened here to him
   and how from woe his mind grew dim.
   Right after he had left this hall,
   while I was lowered down the wall
   suddenly I heard him cry,
   'Alas! Alas!' As soon as I
   got down I ran to him; his pain
   had made the man go quite insane.

1300 "It was a most distressing thing
   for he was just about to spring
   into the water. Were my wit
   not sharp enough to hinder it,
   he would have drowned before my eyes;
   I stopped him with some hurried lies.
   I gave him cheerful news from you
   which brought him to himself anew.

1302 "I counselled him to go and see
   where groom and horses then might be;
   we found them all where they had been.
   As we came back to them again
   I told him more things you had said,
   whatever came into my head.
   I told him you had made it clear,
   in twenty days he must be here.

1303   "I also told him that you bade
        me let him know your heart was sad
        since you had made him go away.
        I said, you couldn't let him stay
        for fear a lady here might tell—
        the one you didn't know so well;
        because of her you must be on
        your guard, but she would soon be gone.

1304   "Thus did I lie to him of you,
        I didn't know what else to do
        because I feared that in despair
        he might do something foolish there
        which he could never more recall.
        But I must tell you once for all:
        if you continue so unkind
        to him, he soon may change his mind.

1306   "I must return to him and say
        what you intend without delay.
        For at St. Pölten he will be,
        where he will serve you gallantly.
        They have arranged a tournament
        and, in your service, he too went
        to prove he can be knightly still
        and honor you with strength and skill."

1307   The good one spoke, "He should not carry
        so sad a look for were he merry
        he'd have more luck. I may be dumb
        but still I know what's wearisome.
        No knight who has a mournful face
        will ever win a lady's grace.
        Whene'er a woman is sad at heart
        because of love, you've not been smart.

1308   "What happened here made quite a show
        when he forgot his manners so
        that he should piteously cry out
        'Alas! Alas!' and really shout
        till he was heard. The watchman went
        down quickly from the battlement
        and through the castle halls to tell
        that he had heard the devil yell.

1309   "They had to ask him when and where.
He spoke, 'See, by the wall down there
I heard the devil loudly roar,
"Alas! Alas! Forever more."
The way he bounded to the lake
was quite enough to make me quake
but then I almost died of fright
when his companion came in sight.'

1310   "And everywhere the watchman said,
'You should have seen the way he fled.
He almost tore the rocks along,
I can't imagine what was wrong.
I prayed that God would guard me well
and bade the devil go to hell.
I ne'er before was so aghast
and never ever prayed so fast.'

1311   "Would you have ever thought your brave
and valiant knight would so behave?
Who lets his knighthood count so small
is really not a man at all.
How could this worthy knight go wailing
just like a woman who is ailing;
and, if he had been recognized,
from that time on he'd been despised."

1312   The courier answered, "I admit,
he had a painful time of it.
So clouded was his reasoning
that life itself meant not a thing.
He'd be already in his grave
had I not managed then to save
him with reports that I contrived,
without which he'd have not survived.

1313   "I've never seen a love so strong
and never known a knight to long
so urgently as he for you;
you can be sure that this is true.
I know that he's of such a mind
that, if you are not soon more kind,
he well may sicken in his prime
and pass away before his time."

1314
"Messenger, when you return,
pray tell your lord, if he would earn
my love then he must take for me
a journey far across the sea.
If God will bring him back again
I promise you that I will then
reward this knight so lovingly
he'll have great joy because of me.

1316
"I'll give myself as his reward;
no woman ever gave her lord
or knight in truth a better pay
than he'll receive. Now you must say:
when he returns from this crusade
as wages he'll at once be paid
with me, and nothing shall he lack—
and, after all, he may come back."

1317
"I'll let him know of your request
and I am sure he'll not protest.
He's told me often heretofore
that he could ask for nothing more
than that you'd give him deeds to dare;
of this I'm sure you were aware.
He'll serve you now as in the past
and faithfully while life shall last."

1318
The page then left and went straight on
to Wasserberg where I had gone
after the tournament was through.
A lot of spears were broke in two
in honor of many a lady fair
by the noble knights who gathered there.
And quite a few of those who came
won by their valor lasting fame.

1319
The messenger found me where I sat
with other men. To have a chat
we went where no one else was near.
I spoke, "Now you must let me hear
all that my lady fair commands
and what to hope for at her hands.
If she will grant me what is right
my heart will once again be light."

1320   He spoke, "I'll tell you what I heard.
The noble lady sends you word
that you have never earned the prize
of love with deeds of any size.
She wants that you go journeying
to honor her. If God should bring
you safely through the pilgrimage
you'll get whate'er you want as wage.

1321   "The lady wishes you to fare
across the sea. In truth, I swear,
if you will do her will, she said,
the trip will stand you in good stead.
Indeed she promises to give
herself as long as she may live,
and what belongs to her alone
you can dispose of as your own."

1322   I said, "Her wish shall be fulfilled
and all besides she may have willed.
There is no obstacle which I
can't overcome and I shall die
or earn myself a lover's pay,
and this in such a knightly way
that she at last in charity
will grant a woman's love to me.

1323   "I'll do whatever she may ask,
be it a great or little task.
How glad I am that she's employed
me as her knight! I'm overjoyed!
There is no trip so long or hard
I would not take for her regard
and nothing else I wouldn't do.
All that I've said, my friend, is true."

1324   He spoke, "I don't like this at all.
You know, of course, there will befall
you often pain and misery.
If you should sail across the sea
it well may be your death indeed
and then might come the greatest need:
that you'd lose out on paradise,
which would be much too great a price.

1325   "No man should make a pilgrimage
to win a lovely woman's wage.
We do this only for our Lord;
He also gives us our reward.
Who journeys for a woman's pay
and perishes along the way
will surely find his soul is lost.
You must consider, sir, the cost."

1326   I answered him, "God is so good,
with sympathetic fatherhood,
and such a noble, lofty mind.
Who serves with honor womankind
need never fear that He'll object.
He wants that we should not neglect
to serve them; that is His design.
This is the truth, O friend of mind.

1328   "Forever more shall I be glad
that my so lovely lady bade
me take the trip in her employ
for I have served her since a boy
without her thanking me a bit.
If I should hesitate with it—
now that my lady's given me
a task—'t would seem quite cowardly."

1329   "Since you're to follow her request
(although I do not think it best)
send someone now and tell her so.
She'll be delighted, as I know.
I'll gladly be your messenger
for I've been well received by her.
The lady's temperament is such,
this news will please her very much."

1332   I left him and it wasn't long
till I'd composed another song.
I rhymed a little book beside
and in its verses I replied
that her command would be obeyed.
More loving verse has ne'er been made
than that I put into this book
in which my lady was to look.

1333 With song and booklet he bestrode
his horse and speedily he rode
to bring them to my lady fair.
He got a hearty welcome there.
She spoke, "Good youth, tell me, I pray
does he intend to earn his pay
by going to that distant land
and thus fulfilling my command?"

1334 "He sends me, lady, here to you.
His heart's desire is just to do
you service; nothing will he shun
and everything be gladly done.
He's ready for the pilgrimage—
for this I'll pledge my soul as gage—
and is quite happy. It is plain,
no task he does for you is pain.

1335 "He sent to you, my lady dear,
by me this little booklet here
and sent a song, both new and gay.
He asked me when I rode away
to put them both into your hand.
The booklet lets you understand,
he'll make the journey 'cross the sea
for you with constant loyalty."

1337 She took them and when she had read
all that the little booklet said
she found it pleased her very well.
And this is why I now can tell
you that my lady good and wise
read with bright and shining eyes
without delay and greatly cheered
the page on which the song appeared.

1338 When she had read it to the end
she went at once back to my friend
and spoke, "I always shall accord
my thanks, and rightly, to your lord
because he thinks so well of me
that he will do and eagerly
whate'er I ask. That does him good
and I'll reward him as I should.

1339
"Ask of him that he prepare
to make the journey and with care
so that when I shall let him know
he will be ready and can go.
I want to see your lord again
and will arrange a time ere then.
He needn't be concerned thereby;
as I'm a woman, it's no lie."

1341
He left the lady and returned,
but I had travelled on, he learned.
'T was in Vienna that he found
me where I'd gone to look around.
I saw there many a pretty maid
and lovely lady, well arrayed,
and thoroughly enjoyed the sight;
it makes one's heart feel warm and light.

1342
When I beheld the messenger
I welcomed him and asked of her.
He let me know without delay
all that she wanted him to say.
I was prepared for nothing less
and did not lack in faithfulness.
It pleased me so that she'd consent
to see me once before I went.

1345
In tournaments the summer through
I jousted and it's surely true
that I had tied my helmet on
a lot of times ere it was gone.
With tilts I served my lady fair
most willingly and everywhere
until the winter came once more
and all the tourneying was o'er.

1346
"Good Lord, when will it be," I thought,
"till she for whom I've often fought
sends me the message I await?
How am I going to know the state
after these months of her regard?
To wait around is pretty hard;
I'd like to hear from her somehow —
would God, a messenger came now!"

1349

She had somebody go and find
my messenger and was so kind
to quickly send him on to me;
he told me all and faithfully.
The message that he brought was such
that I'm afraid I'll say too much
and so I'll stop ere something slips
for chivalry must close my lips.

1350

But that which afterwards befell
is something I'm allowed to tell.
The lady said, I shouldn't take
the distant journey for her sake;
the virtuous and lovely dear
wanted me to stay right here.
My lover's sorrow now was gone —
and then the summer too came on.

1351

My heart was happy and at ease;
I sang two summer melodies,
a march and then another song.
I'd been an orphan for so long
but joy can make the spirit whole —
I felt it in me, and my soul
could barely hold its secret bliss.
Now hear! The verses go like this:

THE SIXTEENTH IS A MARCH

He who with honor would pass the time gaily,
would know true delight and enjoy himself daily
should faithfully serve a fair lady of station
for love's compensation.
Its sweetness and splendor
will only surrender
to those kind and tender.

Who courts as a knight and hopes for successes
must give heart and hand and the goods he possesses,
but love will reward him with wealth beyond measure,
so great is her treasure.
She honors, appeases
her pupil and eases
his care as she pleases.

Knighthood demands both good manners and daring,
dishonor, deceit, and its fellows forswearing,
for God can't endure in his service the babble
of such wretched rabble.
His men must endeavor
to find honor ever
and infamy never.

Malice and coarseness, ill nature and scheming
to neither the shield nor the helmet is seeming,
for knighthood's a roof that no evil can cover.
Its glance shall discover
the honorless, fearful,
the frightened, half-tearful
where brave men are cheerful.

High-minded ladies, remember with favor
the faithful companion whose heart will not waver.
Love him in your thoughts and with all your affection
that thus your protection
may keep with the power
of love him each hour
from griefs that devour.

Through no fault of mine is the lady offended,
though I am her knight and for her have contended.
And now for protection from anger and sorrow
no shield can I borrow
but one: I still love her
and think kindly of her.
None else is above her.

I'll battle with patience her warlike resistance,
opposing her anger with guileless insistence.
Protected because I am faithful and loyal,
all falsehood I'll foil.
My battle attire
against her dread fire
is constant desire.

1352   Singing this song with heart so light
that summer many a gallant knight
went jousting, that was their way of life;
they served their ladies with this strife.
Believe me when I say to you,
there were tournaments the summer through
in every country, here and there.
I didn't miss a one, I swear.

1360   The summer was very summery
and full of summer gaiety.
It grew in summer's strength and power
but still was squandered, hour by hour,
for ladies with chivalric sport.
The noble knights of every court
used up their weapons tourneying
as if the spears weren't worth a thing.

1361   That summer the lady did to me
an awful thing. If it might be
a knight could tell to you this tale
the honest folks would help him wail
that a lady could ever so offend
and wound her faithful knight and friend.
Her action was so mean and small
I never could lament it all.

1362   When with hoarfrost, cold and keen,
the fall destroyed the forest green
and when the heath had lost its gay
attire which it had donned in May
of flowers—every hue and kind—
and when the summer had declined
and stealthily had fled away,
I sang this melancholy lay:

THE TWENTIETH DANCE TUNE

You noble ladies, so refined and lovely, take my part;
before you all do I accuse the mistress of my heart
for she has robbed me so of joy and left me only pain
that because of her I must   evermore complain.

I grieve that she'll not recognize my service, as is right,
although I've served her long and truly like a faithful knight.
That she is praised so highly everywhere by many a tongue
is because I've spread her fame   with the songs I've sung.

I charge my lady with committing theft and robbery,
for it is robbery and theft (what other could it be?)
that she should seize my happiness without declaring war
and deprive my heart of joys,   all for evermore.

I say she is a robber and is guilty of a theft
so great I'll ne'er replace the things of which I am bereft.
If she should give me back enjoyment, which she can and may,
yet imagine what I've lost: many a lovely day.

Because of her I suffer more than I can tell or share
from agonizing, yearning pangs which secretly I bear.
Alas! Alas, that she was born to cause me such distress,
she whose love I most of all   wanted to possess.

Were I not silenced by good manners and by hopes of love,
Then you'd believe, because of all the things she robbed me of
(should I reveal my longing heart and give each crime a name),
that the color of her face   would turn red with shame.

If anyone can reconcile us this would please me so
I'd not be angry anymore nor burdened down with woe,
no one would hear me say of her a word of censure then
and, whate'er she later does,   this, at least, has been.

1363   When my lady heard this song
she wouldn't try to right the wrong
but did a thing which hurt a lot
though I shall never tell you what.
Even today and more and more
with suffering my heart is sore;
I won't reveal the reason why
but keep her secret till I die.

1364   Alas, that she would do this thing!
Alas, that I should ever sing
of her in anger as I've done,
so that long after many a one
condemned this book and also me
who did not know the cruelty
with which my honest love was spurned,
nor with what deeds my wrath was earned.

1365   Since she continued these affronts
I gave up serving her at once
and turned away both mind and heart.
Who from long service does not part
when one gives no reward, nor can,
is really quite a foolish man.
My service went for nought or less—
I sang this song in bitterness:

THE TWENTY-FIRST DANCE TUNE

O to lose and to regret
that which I cannot forget
evermore!
Joy and all my better days—
gone with melancholy lays.
Wounded sore,
I must bear
life given o'er to grieving care:
death is less
than such distress.

There my service was to be
with such constant loyalty
through the years.
Still no pay will she accord
and no prospect of reward.
O my tears!
O! and O!
Had I hopes, as long ago,
I could then
laugh again.

She once filled me with delight
when she let me be her knight
and for life.
I did not complain a bit
at that time, I must admit
without strife.
But so small
is the thanks which she lets fall
that we're poor —
both — that's sure.

Many years, I see with pain,
I have squandered all in vain
for someone
who can never fully pay
me for just a single day
that is done,
since her mind
is no more so good and kind
as when she
conquered me.

She was beautiful and true,
she was lovely through and through
when I chose
her to be the lady fair
whom I honored everywhere,
as she knows.
Then her name
was exalted without shame;
later on
thanks was gone.

1366   Thus she discovered from this song
       that, though I'd served her well and long,
       I would not serve her anymore.
       Alas for this! Alas therefor,
       that she should deal to me the blow
       for which I'd have to leave her so
       and that it ever might occur
       to me to speak so ill of her.

1367   Now tell me if you think I had
       good reason to be very sad
       that I could not be reconciled
       to one I'd worshipped as a child.
       I had to tell her thanklessness
       though I'd have suffered less distress
       if I had perished, I believe.
       Such loss and pain was mine to grieve.

1368   No gracious ladies, I know well,
       will censure me because I tell
       how much my lady did me ill.
       If it depended on my will
       to keep it secret that I'd do.
       No one should claim that I'm untrue.
       She well deserves that I have turned
       from her; it's what her deeds have earned.

1376   I did not scold her anymore
       nor did I serve her as before,
       and after what she did to me
       I was a while quite lady-free
       down to the bottom of my heart.
       But I could not neglect my art
       nor leave off singing women's praise.
       I sang of love and happy days:

In the warm and fragrant Maytime
when the woods are dressed in green
through the happy hours of daytime
all that loves in pairs is seen.
Every heart is filled with bliss
and the spring was made for this.

Loving pairs in pleasant hours
soon are free from all distress;
in the hearts of both there flowers
all the season's happiness.
Sorrow love cannot abide
when two loves are side by side.

When two loving hearts are plighted
faithfully without deceit,
when the two are so united
that their love must be complete,
they are joined by God to capture
all that life can hold of rapture.

Constant love is *minne*. Truly
love and *minne* are the same.
I cannot distinguish duly
ought between them but the name
nor can tell the two apart.
Love is *minne* in my heart.

Find a heart that does not vary,
constant love and constant mind,
then with grief you can be merry.
Constant love is good and kind
and to constant hearts will give
constant pleasure while they live.

If I ever found enduring
love then I would surely be
always loyal, with it curing
all the cares that come to me.
Faithless love will never do,
I must find a love that's true.

BIBLIOGRAPHY

The following works have been consulted. Further information concerning most of these works can be found in

Carl von Kraus, ed. *Deutsche Liederdichter des 13. Jahrhunderts*, vol. II (Tübingen, 1958), pp. 519-520.

The following abbreviation has been used in the Bibliography: *ZfdA*, *Zeitschrift für deutsches Altertum und deutsche Literatur*.

Abert, A. "Das Nachleben des Minnesangs im liturgischen Spiel," *Musikforschung*, I (1948), 95-105.

Arens, Hans. *Ulrichs von Lichtenstein "Frauendienst." Untersuchungen über den höflichen Sprachstil*. Leipzig, 1939.

Review by Arthur Witte, *Literaturblatt für germanische und romanische Philologie*, VII-VIII (1942), 190-196.

Bartsch, Karl and Wolfgang Golther, eds. *Deutsche Liederdichter des 12.-14. Jahrhunderts*. Berlin, 1928, pp. lvii-lviii.

Bechstein, Reinhold, ed. *Ulrich's von Liechtenstein Frauendienst*. 2 vols. Leipzig, 1888.

Review by Anton Schönbach, *Deutsche Literatur Zeitung*, IX (1888), 1112-1114.

Becker, Anton. "Der Weg der Venusfahrt in Niederösterreich," *Monatsblatt des Vereins für Landeskunde von Niederösterreich*, XXIV (1925), 34-43.

Becker, Reinhold. *Ritterliche Waffenspiele nach Ulrich von Lichtenstein*. Programm des Dürener Realprogymnasiums, No. 458. Düren, 1887.

Becker, Reinhold. *Wahrheit und Dichtung in Ulrich von Lichtensteins Frauendienst*. Halle, 1888.

Beckh-Widmanstetter, L. von. *Ulrichs von Liechtenstein, des Minnesängers, Grabmal auf der Frauenburg*. Graz, 1871.

Beckh-Widmanstetter, L. von. "Das Grabmal auf der Frauenburg," *Tagespost*. Graz, No. 274 (Oct. 13, 1871).

Bodmer, J. J. and J. J. Breitinger, eds. *Sammlung von Minnesingern aus dem schwäbischen Zeitpunkte*. Vol. II. Zürich, 1759, pp. 24-46.

Boor, Helmut de. *Geschichte der deutschen Literatur*. Vol. II. München, 1953, pp. 337-346. Vol. III. München, 1957, pp. 313-319.

Bouterwek, Friedrich. *Geschichte der Poesie und Beredsamkeit seit dem Ende des 13. Jahrhunderts*, IX. Göttingen, 1812.

Brecht, Walther. "Ulrich von Liechtenstein als Lyriker," *ZfdA*, XLIX (1908), 1-122.

Review by Anton Schönbach, *Allgemeines Literaturblatt*, XVI (1907), 749-752.

Bruder, Annemarie. *Studien zu Ulrich von Lichtensteins "Frauendienst."* Diss. Freiburg, 1923.

Bub, Felix. *Beiträge zur Genealogie und Geschichte der steierischen Liechtensteine*. Graz, 1902.

Ehrismann, Gustav. "Die Grundlagen des ritterlichen Tugendsystems," *ZfdA*, LVI (1918), 137-216.

Ehrismann, Gustav. *Geschichte der deutschen Literatur bis zum Ausgang des Mittelalters*. Vol. II, 2. München, 1935, pp. 262-265.

Falke, Jacob. *Geschichte des fürstlichen Hauses Liechtenstein*. Vol. I. Wien, 1868, pp. 57-124.

Falke, Jacob. "Ein alter Grabstein," *Tagespost*. Graz, No. 267 (Oct. 6, 1871).

Gennrich, Friedrich, *Troubadours, Trouvères, Minnesang und Meistergesang*. Köln, 1960, p. 71.

Goedeke, Karl, ed. *Grundriss zur Geschichte der deutschen Dichtung*. Vol. I. Dresden, 1894, pp. 168-170.

Görner, Otto. "Ulrich von Lichtenstein in Zerbst," *Mitteldeutsche Blätter für Volkskunde*, V (1930), 33-48.

Grimme, Friedrich. "Beiträge zur Geschichte der Minnesänger II," *Germania*, XXXII (1887), 411-427.

Grimme, Friedrich. "Zum Leben Ulrichs von Lichtenstein," *Germania*, XXXV (1890), 406-407.

Hagen, Friedrich von der, ed. *Minnesinger: Deutsche Liederdichter des 12. 13. und 14. Jahrhunderts*, 5 vols. Leipzig, 1838-1861.
  Vol. II, pp. 32-62. Vol. III, pp. 657-661. Vol. IV, pp. 321-405.

Haupt, Moriz. "Urkundliches zu Mittelhochdeutschen Dichtern," *ZfdA*, VII (1849), 168-169.

Hauptmann, Gerhart. *Ulrich von Lichtenstein. Komödie*. Berlin, 1939.

Höfler, Otto. "Ulrichs von Liechtenstein Venusfahrt und Artusfahrt," *Studien zur deutschen Philologie des Mittelalters*. Ed. Richard Kienast. Heidelberg, 1950, pp. 131-152.

Hösele, Alfred. "Ulrich von Lichtenstein. Der Roman eines Minnesängers," *Jahresbericht des Gymnasiums Carolinum-Augustineum*. Graz, 1954, 3-11.

Huisman, J. A. *Neue Wege zur dichterischen und musikalischen Technik Walthers von der Vogelweide*. Utrecht, 1950, p. 147.

Kalchberg. "Ulrich von Lichtenstein. Geschichtlich untersucht," *Wöchentliche Nachrichten für Freunde der Geschichte, Kunst und Gelahrtheit des Mittelalters*, I (1816), 47-50.
  II (1816), 231-234.

Knorr, Karl. *Über Ulrich von Lichtenstein. Quellen und Forschungen zur Sprach- und Culturgeschichte*, Vol. IX (Strassburg, 1875).
  Review by Otto Behaghel, *Germania*, XXI (1876), 434-436.

Kosch, Wilhelm. *Deutsches Literatur-Lexikon*. Vol. IV. Bern & München, 1958, pp. 3084-3085.

Kracher, Alfred. "Der steierische Minnesang," *Zeitschrift des historischen Vereins für Steiermark*, XLVII (1956), 123-137.

Kraus, Carl von, ed. *Deutsche Liederdichter des 13. Jahrhunderts*. 2 Vols. Tübingen, 1952–1958. Vol. I, pp. 428-495. Vol. II, pp. 519-558.

Kuhn, Hugo. *Minnesangs Wende*. Tübingen, 1952. *Hermaea*. Vol. I, pp. 85-87.

Kummer, Karl F., ed. *Die poetischen Erzählungen des Herrand von Wildonie und die kleinen innerösterreichischen Minnesinger*. Wien, 1880, pp. 21-26, 47-52.

Lachmann, Karl, ed. *Ulrich von Lichtenstein. Mit Anmerkungen von Theodor von Karajan*. Berlin, 1841.

Langenbucher, Hellmuth. *Das Gesicht des deutschen Minnesangs und seine Wandlungen*. Heidelberg, 1930, pp. 69-70.

Lichtenstein, Franz. Review of: Felix Niedner, *Das Deutsche Turnier im XII. und XIII. Jahrhundert. Anzeiger für deutsches Altertum*, VIII (1882), 14-19.

Lind, K. "Ulrich's von Lichtenstein, des Minnesängers Grabmal auf der Frauenburg," *Mitteilungen der kaiserlichen königlichen Zentralkommission für Denkmalpflege*, XVII (1872), 102-103.

Loehr, Maja. "Die Grabplatte auf der steirischen Frauenburg und die Ruhestätte Ulrichs von Liechtenstein," *Mitteilungen des Instituts für österreichische Geschichtsforschung*, LXV (1957), 53-70.

Lucas, Wilhelm. *Das Adjektiv bei Ulrich von Lichtenstein*. Diss. Greifswald, 1914.

Lunzer, J. "Steiermark in der deutschen Heldensage," *Sitzungsberichte der Akademie der Wissenschaften in Wien*, CCIV (1929), 1-196.

Millot, Claude François. *Histoire Littéraire Des Troubadours*, III. Paris, 1774, pp. 127-128.

Milnes, Humphrey. "Ulrich von Lichtenstein and the Minnesang," *German Life and Letters*, XVII (1963-1964), 27-43.

Minis, Cola. "Ulrich von Lichtenstein," *Die Deutsche Literatur des Mittelalters. Verfasser-lexikon*. Vol. v. Ed. Karl Langosch. Berlin, 1955, pp. 1098-1099.

Misch, Georg. *Geschichte der Autobiographie*. Vol. iv, 1. Frankfurt a. M., 1967, pp. 433-437.

Morgan, Bayard Quincy. *A Critical Bibliography of German Literature in English Translation, 1481-1927*. Stanford, 1938, p. 491.

Morgan, Bayard Quincy. *A Critical Bibliography of German Literature in English Translation. Supplement, 1928-1955*. New York & London, 1965, p. 486.

Müller, Günther. "Strophenbindung bei Ulrich von Lichtenstein," *ZfdA*, LX (1923), 33-69.

Neumann, Friedrich. "Ulrich von Lichtensteins Frauendienst. Eine Untersuchung über das Verhältnis von Dichtung und Leben," *Zeitschrift für Deutschkunde*, XL (1926), 373-386.

Nigg, Marianne. *Zum Gedächtnis an den Minnesänger und Dichter Ritter Ulrich von Lichtenstein zu seinem 700. Geburtsjahre*. Korneuburg, 1899.

Ortner, M. "Ulrich von Lichtenstein und Steinmar," *Germania*, XXXII (1887), 120-125.

Ottokars Österreichische Reimchronik. Ed. Josef Seemüller. *Monumenta Germaniae Historica, Deutsche Chroniken*. Vol. v, pts. 1 & 2. Hannover, 1890-1893, ll. 1971f., 2296f., 5944f., 6002f., 6012f., 6027f., 6059f., 9866f., 9878f., 9905f., 9997f., 10001f., 10015f., 10051f., 10058f., 10539f.

Petzet, Erich and Otto Glauning, eds. *Deutsche Schrifttafeln des IX. bis XVI. Jahrhunderts*. Vol. III. München, 1912, Tafel XXXVI.

Pfaff, Fridrich, ed. *Die Grosse Heidelberger Liederhandschrift*. Heidelberg, 1909, pp. 771-823.

Pfaff, Fridrich, ed. *Der Minnesang des 12.-14. Jahrhunderts*. Vol. I. Stuttgart, 1892, pp. 133-142.

Pfeiffer, Franz, ed. *Die Alte Heidelberger Liederhandschrift*. Hildesheim, 1962, pp. 126-127, 258.

Puff, Rudolf. "Beiträge zur Geschichte des ritterlichen steirischen Sängers Ulrich von Lichtenstein," *Programm des Staatsgymnasiums in Marburg*. Marburg, 1856, pp. 1-11.

Reuschel, H. "Ulrich von Lichtenstein," *Die Deutsche Literatur des Mittelalters. Verfasser-lexikon*. Vol. IV. Ed. Karl Langosch. Berlin, 1953, pp. 584-589.

Rödiger, Max. "Zu Ulrichs von Lichtenstein Büchlein," *ZfdA*, XXII (1878), 380-382.

Ruhemann, Alfred. "Einleitung," *Frauendienst, oder Geschichte und Liebe des Ritters und Sängers Ulrich von Lichtenstein*. Tr. Ludwig Tieck. Volksbibliothek für Kunst und Wissenschaft, Abtlg. Varia, Heft 213. Leipzig, 1885, pp. 1-3.

Rust, Werner. *Freud und Leid in Ulrich von Lichtensteins Frauendienst*. Diss. Greifswald, 1918.

Scherer, Wilhelm and Oskar Walzel. *Geschichte der deutschen Literatur*. 4th ed. Leipzig, 1928, pp. 162-163.

Scherer, Wilhelm "Der Kürenberger," *ZfdA*, XVII (1873), 561-581.

Schlereth, Martha. *Studien zu Ulrich von Lichtenstein*. Diss. Würzburg, 1950.

Schmidt, Erich. *Reinmar von Hagenau und Heinrich von Rugge*. Quellen und Forschungen zur Sprach- und Culturgeschichte. Vol. IV (Strassburg, 1874), pp. 116-120.

Schneider, Karl Ludwig. "Die Selbstdarstellung des Dichters im Frauendienst Ulrichs von Lichtenstein," *Festgabe für Ulrich Pretzel*. Berlin, 1963, pp. 216-223.

Schönbach, Anton. "Zu Ulrich von Lichtenstein," *ZfdA*, XXVI (1882), 307-326.

Schönbach, Anton. "Ulrich von Liechtenstein," *Allgemeine deutsche Biographie*. Vol. XVIII. Leipzig, 1883, pp. 620-623.

Schönbach, Anton. "Zum Frauendienst Ulrichs von Liechtenstein," *Zeitschrift für deutsche Philologie*, XXVIII (1896), 198-226.

Schönbach, Anton. "Zu Ulrich von Liechtenstein," *Anzeiger für deutsches Altertum*, XXIX (1904), 277-278.

Schopf, A. W. "Die Töne Uolrichs von Liehtenstein [sic]," *Viertes Programm des K. K. kathol. Gymnasiums zu Pressburg*. Pressburg, 1854, pp. 3-16.

Schröder, Edward. "Herrand von Wildon und Ulrich von Lichtenstein," *Göttinger Nachrichten*, 1923, pp. 33-62.

Schröder, Edward. "Zur Textkritik Ulrich von Lichtensteins," *ZfdA*, LXIX (1932), 323-332.

Silberstein, August. *Denksäulen im Gebiet der Cultur und Literatur*. Wien, 1879, pp. 79-163.

Sprenger, R. "Zu Ulrichs von Lichtenstein Frauendienst," *Germania*, XXXVII (1892), 174-180.

Tieck, Ludwig, tr. *Minnelieder aus dem schwäbischen Zeitalter.* Berlin, 1803, pp. 126–144.

Tieck, Ludwig, tr. *Frauendienst, oder Geschichte und Liebe des Ritters und Sängers Ulrich von Lichtenstein.* Stuttgart & Tübingen, 1812.

Touber, A. H. "Der literarische Charakter von Ulrich von Lichtensteins *Frauendienst,*" *Neophilologus,* LI (1967), 253–262.

Uhland, Ludwig. *Schriften zur Geschichte der Dichtung und Sage.* Vol. V. Stuttgart, 1870, pp. 210–244.

"Alte steierische Gedichtsfunde und Dichter. III. Herr Ulrich von Liechtenstein" (anon.), *Tagespost.* Graz, No. 269 (Nov. 24, 1864).

Utz, Franz. *Das Moralsystem bei Ulrich von Lichtenstein.* Diss. Greifswald, 1920.

Wackernagel, Wilhelm. *Geschichte der deutschen Literatur.* Vol. I, 2. Basle, 1889, p. 285.

"Wandelhalle der Bücherfreunde" (anon.), *Zeitschrift für Bücherfreunde,* XXXVII (1933), 153.

Weinhold, Karl. *Über den Antheil Steiermarks an der Deutschen Dichtkunst des Dreizehnten Jahrhunderts.* Almanach der Akademie der Wissenschaften. Wien, 1860, pp. 18–23.

Werner, Richard Maria. Review of: Ferdinand Michel. *Heinrich von Morungen und die Troubadours. Anzeiger für deutsches Altertum,* VII (1881), 121–151.

Wilmanns, Wilhelm. Review of: Konrad Burdach, *Reinmar der Alte und Walther von der Vogelweide. Ein Beitrag zur Geschichte des Minnesangs. Anzeiger für deutsches Altertum,* VII (1881), 258–273.

Wilmanns, Wilhelm. Review of: Rumpelt, *Das natürliche System der Sprachlaute. Sokrates: Zeitschrift für das Gymnasialwesen,* XXIV (1870), 578–602.

Woratschek, Margareta. *Eine Reimuntersuchung zu Ulrich von Lichtenstein: Frauendienst und Frauenbuch.* Diss. Wien, 1956.

Zahn, "Der Frauenburger Grabstein," *Tagespost.* Graz, No. 279 (Oct. 18, 1871).

Zitzenbacher, Walther, tr. *Ulrich von Liechtenstein. Narr im hohen Dienst.* Graz & Wien, 1958.

Zois, Michelangelo, tr. *Der Frauendienst des Minnesängers Ulrich von Liechtenstein.* Stuttgart, 1924.